Live Your DREAMS

JEAN CRISS

AuthorHouse™ LLC
1663 Liberty Drive
Bloomington, IN 47403
www.authorhouse.com
Phone: 1-800-839-8640

Published by AuthorHouse: 07/16/2014

ISBN: 978-1-4969-1085-1 (sc)
ISBN: 978-1-4969-1086-8 (e)

authorHOUSE®

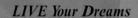

LIVE Your Dreams

Part Three of ***My Pain Woke Me Up*** Trilogy

A story about entrepreneurship; dreaming BIG, living it,
unleashing your inner creativity to make all those dreams come true.

Dedication

My story is first and foremost dedicated to my two teens. I never set sail without taking my eye off my two beautiful children. They continue to be my priority, my love, and inspiration as I watch them grow to become the best they can be, as individuals and young adults. I always remember the many days we made a BIG wish, threw a penny in a pond, blew *bubbles* to make a BIG wish and reach for the sky and *LIVE Our Dreams*—so we are!

I would also like to acknowledge the most positive, inspirational business colleague I've ever met throughout my career. She may not know it but she gave me the courage, confidence and belief in myself that I could '*LIVE My Dreams*' if I truly wanted to pursue all these crazy ideas I had. Her '*positive push*' went such a long way. Even Teri Evans, Deputy Editor of Entrepreneur.com Magazine once told me, "boy you're on fire!" and I owe that to Stella! A big shout out to Stella Grizont, former Managing Director of Ladies Who Launch/NYC Chapter, now Founder of Woopah! - a company that creates immersive play experiences for people at work to feel happier, more creative, and connected. Stella, a Master Graduate in the Science of Applied Happiness and Positive Psychology from UPenn; who knew there was such an esteemed major? I can assert that she not only has earned her ranks, but she applies her knowledge to everything she embraces. Stella, you are just one amazing woman, thank you.

To my dad, the best multi-tasking business entrepreneur I know. Perhaps it has always been in my blood and I'm so grateful to have learned dad's best practices and tips all along the way! Your energy throughout my life and career has been tremendous with proven success and dedication to your 63-year dental practice, building and development businesses and those in the community. Your love for our family has been endless, and you show it in every way. Of course, with the endless love and support of Mom, at our side as well. Thank you both for your inspiration and belief in me. I love you both so very much! And remember Dad, "*don't sweat the small stuff right!*" and "*don't put off tomorrow what you can do today*!" Well spoken.

To my many business friends and colleagues who have shared best business practices and sales successes with me over the years. To name a few, I'd like to acknowledge the following; Steve Lewis, a business colleague and admired friend for the past few years. Steve has been very supportive of my dreams: positive, helpful, and encouraging. His visionary prowess and superb leadership far exceeds those that are driven in this digital era, bar none. We can all learn something each day from great leaders like Steve. Thank you for always being there and sharing such wonderful insight.

To Jim Manzi, who believed in me and saw my talents at an early age when I was still discovering my hidden talents while managing his largest F500 account (General Motors) and before creating his Top 20 national accounts sales program and leading top CEO marketing programs, I was contending with challenging and personal life changes as a young widow simultaneously. Thank you for your kindness and admiration over the years.

To Pat Kenealy who taught me how to manage my first P&L and so much more. The tough, business prowess and savvy mediate business practices that you instilled in me have carried me along from job to job through different industries. Thanks Pat!

To Kelly Conlin for his leadership and belief that I could take on a multi-media corporate ad responsibility simultaneously while holding down the fort with worldwide media, conferences and business unit responsibility for Lotus, I am forever grateful for being thrown into the fire and to have learned the ad-side of the business.

To my dear colleague, Mark Flanagan, who created a senior leadership position for me which required I depart Lotus Development after years of successful sales track record to lead a new ancillary publishing division while managing numerous business partnerships. Your drive, perseverance and continued support over the years has been inspiring.

To Terry Dwyer who was my first publishing and sales director who taught me that '*it's okay if we don't please all the fish in the sea, there's many more out there*', so to speak. Well Terry, you and I know you and I know that you told me that in other words, but they have stuck with me year over year. ☺

To John Kilcullen, who also taught me so much about self-publishing and little did I know I was also learning about the launch of my future new businesses in hind-sight! Thanks John.

To Ellen Freeman, Sarah Fay, David Verklin and the entire Carat-Freeman team, one of my leading media agencies and partner's year over year. With many unchartered industries and categories, we pushed forward with leading-edge solutions and technologies to service our clients with best practices the way I've always known best how to deliver to my clientele. Thank you for your 'ear', your 'shoulder' over the years, and for your on-going friendship and business.

There have been many more leaders that have showed me the ropes, coached or guided me throughout my sales and leadership career. Too many names to mention and for that, I am forever grateful for their dedication and support.

Now as an entrepreneur, to my groups of women media-preneurs, colleagues and solo-preneurs that I have spent endless hours with over these recent years learning new ways in which to collaborate with, supported by fresh ideas, new spirit, and bonding friendships that will last a lifetime, established with healthy boundaries and meaningful praise and memories to cherish in the days ahead. Life becomes meaningless without the bond and sense of true friendship, the gift of life that comes by Living Your Dreams.

Now let's look at my journey and take a leap ahead into my world fulfilled with joy, spirit, creativity, energy and delight that prides my soul. A day in the life of . . . '*moi*.'

While reaching for the STARS knowing that I am now living by my dreams. I have learned more about the magnitude life gives and all that I can share with others. To walk the walk, to feel the ocean breeze calling your name, pulling you in, beyond control, where life challenges you and where you can find your self-less ego, and self-motivation to succeed, and to rise above it all, and reach for the sparkle that you see in the sky. That star gazing at you. Those bubbles re-appear in the sky to wish for something new and wonderful! Perhaps gaze down at you. We learn how to find that rainbow which inspires us each and every day. That's what I've been striving for. It may sound like a dream—well it's actually been my journey to do some things that have been on my mind for quite a while. Thoughts and ideas and now it's time I put them into PLAY.

We've all heard about that great experience of P-L-A-Y lately, right!

Well my PLAY has been as a multi-tasking mediapreneur -- one filled with creative ideas consumed with digital media, social media, advertising, television, publishing, radio, branding, publicity and other innovative marketing and sales services. I started down a path of mapping out numerous ideas, sketching them, and creating my own graphics (and I was never a graphics expert).

Well it wasn't about making a picture perfect image. It was about getting the concepts down on paper and then taking things to the next step. I built my plan, like any new business person would do, before I put it into PLAY.

What you see today is a series of creative media service offerings.

When in the midst of chaos find that stillness within you.

My ideas came from within and it all started here — take a look at http://JeanCrissMedia.com. We'll help you grow your business and *LIVE Your Dreams!*

Entrepreneurship Advice

©Marty Bucella

www.martybucella.com

"Your drug test results show you aren't taking any performance enhancing drugs. Your performance review results shows that maybe you should."

A dear friend once shared this story with me and I'd like to share it with you.

A young lady confidently walked around the room while leading and explaining stress management to an audience with a raised glass of water. Everyone knew she was going to ask the ultimate question, 'half empty or half full?' . . . She fooled them all . . ."How heavy is this glass of water?" she inquired with a smile.

Answers called out ranged from 8 oz. to 20 oz. She replied, "The absolute weight doesn't matter.

It depends on how long I hold it.

If I hold it for a minute, that's not a problem.

If I hold it for an hour, I'll have an ache in my right arm.

If I hold it for a day, you'll have to call an ambulance.

In each case it's the same weight, but the longer I hold it, the heavier it becomes." She continued, "and that's the way it is with stress. If we carry our burdens all the time, sooner or later, as the burden becomes increasingly heavy, we won't be able to carry on."

"As with the glass of water, you have to put it down for a while and rest before holding it again. When we're refreshed, we can carry on with the burden—holding stress longer and better each time practiced.

So, as early in the evening as you can, put all your burdens down. Don't carry them through the evening and into the night . . . Pick them up tomorrow. *(Thanks Susan!)*

1. 'Accept the fact that some days you're the pigeon, and some days you're the statue!'
2. 'Always keep your words soft and sweet, just in case you have to eat them.'
3. 'Always read stuff that will make you look good, if you die in the middle of it.'
4. 'Drive carefully . . . It's not only cars that can be recalled by their Maker.'
5. ' If you can't be kind, at least have the decency to be vague.'
6. 'If you lend someone $20 and never see that person again, it was probably worth it.'
7. 'It may be that your sole purpose in life is simply to serve as a warning to others.'
8. 'Never buy a car you can't push.'(*Okay, I really have to work on this one!*)
9. 'Never put both feet in your mouth at the same time, because then you won't have a leg to stand on.'
10. 'Nobody cares if you can't dance well. Just get up and dance for God's sake.'
11. 'Since it's the early worm that gets eaten by the bird, sleep late.'
12. 'The second mouse gets the cheese.'
13. 'When everything's coming your way, you're in the wrong lane.'
14. 'Birthdays are good for you. The more you have, the longer you live.'
15. 'Some mistakes are too much fun to make only once.'
16. 'We could learn a lot from crayons. Some are sharp, some are pretty and some are dull. Some have weird names and all are different colors, but they all have to live in the same box.'
17. 'A truly happy person is one who can enjoy the scenery on a detour.'
18. 'Have an awesome day and know that someone has thought about you today.'

AND MOST IMPORTANTLY,

19. 'Save the earth . . . . It's the only planet with chocolate!'

Indulge in daydreams
with vision, emotion, your
deepest thoughts, and
your wish(es) shall come
true!

Believing in you is
THE key to success!

HISTORY OF DREAMS

Freud: Dreams as the Road to the Unconscious Mind:

In his book *The Interpretation of Dreams*, Sigmund Freud suggested that the content of dreams is related to wish fulfillment. Freud believed that the manifest content of a dream, or the actually imagery and events of the dream, served to disguise the latent content, or the unconscious wishes of the dreamer.

Freud also described four elements of this process that he referred to as 'dream work':

- **Condensation**—Many different ideas and concepts are represented within the span of a single dream. Information is condensed into a single thought or image.
- **Displacement**—This element of dream work disguises the emotional meaning of the latent content by confusing the important and insignificant parts of the dream.
- **Symbolization**—This operation also censors the repressed ideas contained in the dream by including objects that are meant to symbolize the latent content of the dream.
- **Secondary Revision**—During this final stage of the dreaming process, Freud suggested that the bizarre elements of the dream are reorganized in order to make the dream comprehensible, thus generating the manifest content of the dream.

Jung: Archetypes and the Collective Unconscious:

While Carl Jung shared some commonalities with Freud, he felt that dreams were more than an expression of repressed wishes. Jung suggested that dreams revealed both the personal and collective unconscious and believed that dreams serve to compensate for parts of the psyche that are underdeveloped in waking life. However, later research by Hall discovered that the traits people exhibit while they awake are also expressed in dreams.

Jung also suggested that archetypes such as the anima, the shadow and the animus are often represented symbolic objects or figures in dreams. These symbols, he believed, represented attitudes that are repressed by the conscious mind. Unlike Freud, who often suggested that specific symbols represents specific unconscious thoughts, Jung believed that dreams can be highly personal and that interpreting these dreams involved knowing a great deal about the individual dreamer.

Hall: Dreams as a Cognitive Process:

Calvin S. Hall proposed that dreams are part of a cognitive process in which dreams serve as 'conceptions' of elements of our personal lives. Hall looked for themes and patterns by analyzing thousands of dream diaries from participants, eventually creating a quantitative coding system that divided the content of dreams into a number of different categories.

According to Hall's theory, interpreting dreams requires knowing:
- The actions of the dreamer within the dream
- The objects and figures in the dream
- The interactions between the dreamer and the characters in the dream
- The dream's setting, transitions and outcome

The ultimate goal of this dream interpretation is not to understand the dream, however, but to understand the dreamer.

Domhoff: Dreams as a Reflection of Waking Life:

G. William Domhoff is a prominent dream researcher who studied with Calvin Hall at the University of Miami. In large-scale studies on the content of dreams, Domhoff has found that dreams reflect the thoughts and concerns of a dreamer's waking life. Domhoff suggests a neurocognitive model of dreams in which the process of dreaming results from neurological processes and a system of schemas. Dream content, he suggests, results from these cognitive processes.

Popularizing Dream Interpretation

Since the 1970s, dream interpretation has grown increasingly popular thanks to work by authors such as Ann Faraday. In books such as *The Dream Game*, Faraday outlined techniques and ideas than anyone can use to interpret their own dreams. Today, consumers can purchase a wide variety of books that offer dream dictionaries, symbol guides and tips for interpreting and understanding dreams.

Dream research will undoubtedly continue to grow and generate interest from people interested in understanding the meaning of their dreams. However, dream expert G. William Domhoff recommends that ". . . unless you find your dreams fun, intellectually interesting, or artistically inspiring, then feel free to forget your dreams."[1] Others such as Cartwright and Kaszniak propose that dream interpretation may actually reveal more about the interpreter than it does about the meaning of the dream itself.

References

Domhoff, G.W. (n.d.). The "purpose" of dreaming. http://www.dreamresearch.net

Freud, S. (1900). *The Interpretation of Dreams.*

Jung, Carl (1966). "The Practical Use of Dream-analysis." *The Practice of Psychotherapy: Essays on the Psychology of Transference.*

Hall, C. S. (1953). A cognitive theory of dreams. *The Journal of General Psychology, 49,* 273-282. Domhoff, G.W. (2002). "Toward a Neurocognitive Model of Dreams." *The Scientific Study of Dreams.* Domhoff, G.W. (1996). *Finding meaning in dreams: A quantitative approach.* New York and London: Plenum Press.

Cartwright R.D. & Kaszniak, A. (1991). The social psychology of dream reporting. In S.J. Ellman & J.S. Antrobus (Eds.), *The mind in sleep: Psychology and psychophysiology, (2nd ed.).* New York: Wiley.

"A dream is a work of "art" which requires of the dreamer no particular talent, special training, or technical competence. Dreaming is a creative enterprise in which all may and most do participate."—Clark S. Hall

* * *

"The difference between a dreamer and a visionary is that a dreamer has his eyes closed and a visionary has his eyes open."—Martin Luther King Jr., I Have a Dream

* * *

"Dreaming is at the heart of disruption. Whether we want to disrupt an industry or our personal status quo in order to make that terrifying leap from one learning curve to the next (http://blogs.hbr.org/johnson2012/09/throw-your-life-a- curve.html),(http:// whitneyjohnson.com/disrupt-yourself/), we must dream. The good news is that the casual mechanism for achieving our dreams is always, always, always showing up: and as we show up, our future will too."—Whitney Johnson, HBR Blog Network

Don't shrink your dreams. Super-size your courage and abilities.

Karen Salmansohn
notsalmon.com

MORNING JAVA

Morning Java . . . I start each day with a thought which often wakes me during my sleep or I may think of a new idea during my morning shower and I jot it down.

Whenever it's your time to be creative, let your thoughts take you to new places! Reference them and put them into PLAY.

You will inspire yourself thru self-motivation and others too.

Have your morning coffee! ☺

'A goal is simply a dream with a deadline'—remember that!

　　　　　www.martybucella.com

"Take a seat. The boss never tortures a
soul until after he's had his coffee."

CONTENTS

The End

Disclaimer

This is a non-fiction story about dreams.
As an entrepreneur the only way to succeed is to 'live your dreams'.
Be inspired by whatever drives you and creativity will follow.

By Jean Criss
This is my story

Names in this book may have been changed to protect the privacy of friends and family.

Humorous and graphical illustrations were used to add meaning to my story.
What is life, without humor and inspiration?!

Special thanks to these colleagues...

❖ ***Marty Bucella***, *Cartoonist & Humorous Illustrator (www.martybucella.com)*
❖ ***Randy Glasbergen***, *Cartoonist & Humorous Illustrator (www.glasbergen.com)*
❖ ***Karen Salmansohn***, *Author, Oprah Columnist, Consultant & Designer (www.notsalmon.com)*

Prologue

A survivor's tale of inspiration, achievement, and desire to succeed by living my dreams!

This is the third book in the trilogy series, *My Pain Woke Me Up*, *called* ***LIVE Your Dreams*** *which* was written by being self-motivated to pursue new ideas as an entrepreneur, as an avid risk-taker, adventurous and daring. I explored new ground where I have never traveled before, touched new markets and territory that was previously foreign to me, and unleashed my inner creativity.

I found I was able to do just that by starting at ground zero. I felt as though I was there, at the bottom already, having recently been divorced required that I start a fresh new life for myself, not only personally but in professionally too since I was laid off simultaneously. Since I was diagnosed with Breast Cancer, I started the battle fighting to support this cause and to help find a cure. So much was going on in my personal life that I really needed a boost in my professional life. Where else was there for me to go but 'UP'?

I had fallen deep financially with the divorce and the market, but this book is about the present and the future, and not about the past—you may have already read about some of that in my prior books. So let's focus on how someone picks oneself up off the mat to rebuild their life by making a fresh start with their career, while maintaining a healthy home and heart, and sets sail with healthy boundaries, seeking life-long happiness. Sounds good to me!

I wasn't asking for much right? No, I wasn't. In a world of chaos, and all the negativity that I experienced, I needed to **shift** my world in the utmost positive way with good health, prosperity, and happiness (***BLISS!***). I wanted to live by the meaning of my first book entitled ***BLISS!*** I lived by these 5 letters.

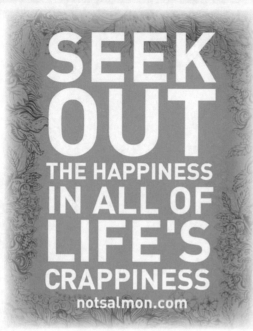

©Marty Bucella

www.martybucella.com

"Judy, I'm bored. Are there any paradigms that need shifting?"

- ✓ Surround myself with happy positive people
- ✓ Associate myself with inspiration an influential people
- ✓ Engulf yourself with life's joys and abundance
- ✓ Encourage collaboration and leadership
- ✓ Be the driving force to get what 'you' want and need; yet deliver what 'they' want and need too!
- ✓ Don't let other's bring you down, ever again! Walk away, if that ever happens again.
- ✓ Rise above it all
- ✓ Keep your head held high
- ✓ Persevere
- ✓ Remember your strengths
- ✓ Build upon them
- ✓ Don't get bogged down in other's nonsense (I believe Steve Job's referred to this as 'Dogma')
- ✓ Aspire to be the best that you can be, and you will
- ✓ Focus on excellence, and commit to excellence
- ✓ Follow your dreams
- ✓ Live by no rules, well, I prefer to call it structure rather than rules or controls
- ✓ Hold people accountable, when appropriate or applicable, apply consequences
- ✓ Live one day at a time

✓ Cherish oneself and one another
✓ Be inspired by great leaders and take at least one piece of advice from each one
✓ Be a sponge and learn something new every day!
✓ Build upon that knowledge
✓ Use your wisdom to drive forces to higher plateaus
✓ Those plateaus will become your foundation or platform for your future
✓ Build a digital platform
✓ Make it your own
✓ Find your niche and put it into PLAY!
✓ Make it your greatest achievement
✓ Multi-task, as we women best do
✓ Utilize multi-media and integrated marketing tools
✓ Don't be afraid to delegate and share resources
✓ Involve others and partner
✓ Partner, partner, and partner!
✓ Seek advice by trusted colleagues, family and friends
✓ Build your business plan
✓ Set sail!
✓ Let go a little
✓ No, let go a lot!
✓ Live, learn, laugh and love (and have great sex too!)
✓ Laugh a lot!
✓ Let's get to work!!
✓ Are you ready?

My self-motivation to succeed came from within, and across many angles, so I put pen to paper and went to work as a fresh new entrepreneur!

Boy, no girl! That sounds great, doesn't it?

No "corporate" world associated with my name. Just little 'ole me in my four corners, living and breathing new ideas! Wow, exhilarating.

Here's how my journey began, enjoy the ride!

"Even though I work from home, it's important to dress appropriately. For conference calls, I wear my best bathrobe. For sales calls, I wear my lucky slippers. And on casual Friday, I go commando."

DREAM IT!
(Think BIG)

I was always a fan of fashion and jewelry, my mom taught me to dress well with stylish clothing, designer labels and name brands. So after I had my two children—one was an infant, and the other was a toddler by now, I was in a failed marriage trying to keep my head above water when I realized . . . '*there is more to life out there isn't there?*'

I worked full-time in media and digital sales, traveled frequently, in and out of state, maintained our home, children, coordinated a live-out nanny, and commuted to two sales offices across two states weekly. Boston and NYC was my weekly routine at that time, and I traveled nationally on occasion, while managing an $18M technology magazine in advertising sales for a large national publishing company in Manhattan while living in Rhode Island (in between the two sales offices). The job required that I entertain clients weekly—over lunch, dinner, business meetings, breakfast meetings, and at industry events. I was used to the hustle and bustle of the days work and morning and evening traffic.

My spouse traveled weekly as he managed out-of-state beer distributors and key accounts for his employer, commuting to Connecticut, Boston, New York, Rhode Island and New Hampshire primarily, with an occasional trip to the Midwest or down south on business. I often felt abandoned with all my household responsibilities but with my independent upbringing I managed and knew how to handle a home solo, almost like a solo-entrepreneur then, juggling the day job which goes with the territory of a working mom and persevered with the night job too. It's what most multi-tasking working women learn to do; you just seem to pull through.

So as I put my pedal to the metal and charged forward, I learned how to handle, most of this on my own. My family lived in the Midwest so it was primarily up to me to figure it all out. The daily schedule: day care, pre-school, after school activities, meals, doctor's appointments, etc. Family life was busy needless to say.

Since my family lived in the Midwest after I moved to the East Coast, and my in-laws were scattered throughout the

Northeast, we had to figure it out. So while I could not rely on local family to pitch in to babysit or lend a helping hand with the kids, it became a stressful time with much responsibility for me. Though I hired many baby sitters and live-out nannies along the way, it still was exhausting.

During the early morning waking hours, I started a hobby to burn off some excess steam and energy! You might say what excess energy right? Well yes, I did yoga and Pilates regularly but I am not referring to that. I taught myself how to bead jewelry!

I became fascinated at the local retail stores with all the "baubles" and wanted to explore. As I mentioned, I always loved to shop high fashion, styles of all sorts, and so I learned how to craft. I purchased all the proper tools, wires, sterling silver clasps, semi-precious stones—gorgeous stones (my taste has always been expensive, thanks Mom!) and away I went. I glanced at the '*How to books*' but I didn't need them. I had learned how to knit, sew, even crochet and needle point as a little girl, thanks again to Mom. Beading seemed so similar, I just jumped right in.

After I mastered creating a bracelet or two on my own, I ventured into taking a class locally in Caldwell, New Jersey, where I officially learned how to bead earrings.

This was fascinating! After that it was smooth sailing. I was well on my own way to becoming an "*Entrepreneur*" but I didn't know it back then. Never assigned a title to it; it became my new" *hobby*".

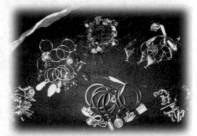

I made bracelets, earrings, necklaces—long and short, beaded rings, ankle bracelets, then branched out with silk belts with beaded fringe, wine charms, beer charms (for the *ex* and our home parties), small purses and bags, sand art vases, key chains, book markers, and so on. Yes, I had so much fun! When I traveled to the Caribbean and to the French Riviera on vacation one summer, I came up with new bauble ideas—like the sand art vases with stones and shells, colorful sand and flowers, and just kept doing different things. I beaded at nighttime as that was my *R 'n R (rest and relaxation)*. I would bead after I cooked dinner for the kids and cleaned up, and then bead again while watching TV, until I passed out for the night.

If I could not sleep, I would get up and bead some more in the early dawn. It was my nighttime therapy before I became a writer. I was so unhappy in my marriage no one knew it but me. I had so much nervous energy that beading became my *self-help therapy*, and I cumulated so much merchandise that I did not know what to do with all of it!

I created home shows to start selling my baubles line, and the neighbor ladies invited me into their homes to host '*wine and bauble*' parties for **LNO**—Ladies Night Out celebrations. They also suggested I join the town Street Fairs so I decided to tour Northern and Central, New Jersey that first year. I bought a 10' x 10' pop-up tent and traveled around the communities with the local Chambers. While I did that for one summer at our local town Street Festivals, the heat became unbearable with the long days away from the kids, and it was too much to bear for what I earned. I also would return home to an unhappy spouse. No matter if I was enjoying what I was doing during the day, the pleasure was sucked right out of me the minute I walked through those doors. I decided my mini launch "craft" business wasn't worth the grief I would receive on the back-end. It also was not worthwhile financially since cash flow was only at break even and not yet profitable. It was hardly worth the time and effort with the added grief on the home front. Although the pure enjoyment and distraction, was well worth it and the business experience was a huge plus I must admit. I learned so much in a short period of time. I just could not afford to continue then.

I chose to participate at a women's club in town to sell my jewelry line as a new venture. The first event was a Holiday Bazaar at Twin Maples sponsored by The Fortnightly Club of Summit, in Summit, New Jersey. What a small world. The funny thing is that I lost touch with this women's organization for years during the downfall of my marriage and now I am back involved there, serving on their Board, as PR Chair, and I am delighted to be involved working with so many smart and talented women again! It is a refreshing change putting all the negative things behind me and focusing on the positive, inspirational things with people who encourage me. Putting those dreams back into PLAY my way.

****

The next successful event was held at The Grand Summit Hotel where women flocked to this annual Holiday Bazaar from all over nearby towns and that was when I realized I may be well on my way to something very fulfilling while 'living my dreams'. I received front page Press in our local community paper and had strong merchandise sales for one night. That pile of inventory had finally moved! In fact, both events were such a success I moved boat loads of inventory. It was all good and proceeds supported women's charity, even better. I wasn't sure where I wanted to go with the business next, but kept driving it forward.

The business required that I put in time primarily on the weekends, since I worked full-time during the business day (week days) for a cable television company, traveling to and fro throughout New Jersey each day, I didn't have a minute to think about this jewelry business with my two small children at home. I just knew I had to move that inventory!

©Marty Bucella   www.martybucella.com

"I can't get by on this allowance. You're forcing me to borrow from China."

My adorable tikes (helpers)!
Baubles and more at The
Grand Summit Hotel,
Summit, NJ
'Holiday Bazarre'

Baubles, Art & Accessories

Jewelry Pouches, Fashion Belts & Napkin Rings

As I continued to build my inventory I looked for someone to sell my merchandise because I just didn't have the time to do that anymore by myself. I really did not want to begin traveling nationally to trade shows to market these items, or anything like that, especially with small children at home and an unsettled marriage. Those events would have been the natural progression or step for me to take in the retail fashion or design industry but with two young toddlers at home to care for, that was out of the question, while I was the bread winner and responsible for holding down the fort. The broken marriage was my top priority so. to stay close to home to support my children and entire family was the main focus.

Beaded Baubles, LLC became my pre-launch, first self—owned business as an entrepreneur, and I loved it!

"When I said you could name your salary,
I meant you could give it a name."

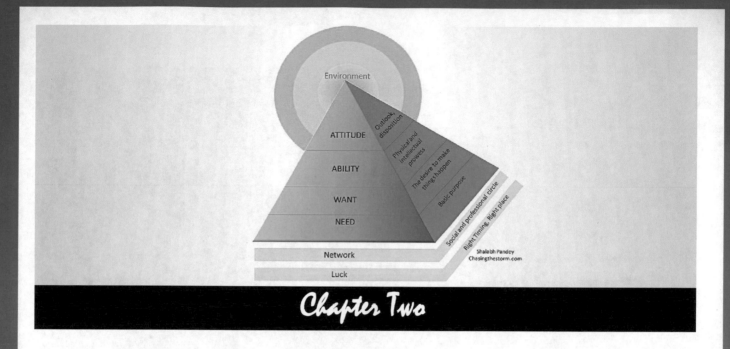

Chapter Two

MINI-LAUNCH—LLC
(Idea phase)

One day I met a woman who informed me of this small store in Chester, New Jersey where they catered to crafters of all sorts. I drove there to meet with the owners and showed them my trade and craft. It was an exciting time for me as a new entrepreneur. Instead of pitching cable TV networks or advertising, I was finally pitching something homegrown! I added sterling silver tags to some of the jewelry pieces that said "*made with love*" or "*made especially for you*". One day, I figured if I ever made enough money to made it 'big', I'd create the silver charm that said "*designed by Jean*" or something like that. But instead, I just created business cards instead that said that, **"Beaded Baubles, LLC"** . . ."**Designed by Jean**" and tied those to each piece of jewelry. Before you knew it, the owners loved my jewelry and all the other types of merchandise that I had designed and created. They convinced me to "rent" a fairly large end-cap unit, called a POP (point of purchase) display, so I did!

Purses and such

This was all so new to me but I was game! It was an exciting time, and this was my first entre' into being a true entrepreneur. I moved my baubles to this store in 2001—a few years before I started in the cable television business in 2004. Since I had a regular paying job then, I decided I could not hold any more home shows at my neighbors homes or at mine once I returned back to work full-time. However, once in a while, I would fulfill special orders for friends to create a unique memento upon request — you may recall those silver bracelets for newborn babies that were especially designed with your children's name(s) on them? Square sterling peg, lettered beaded bracelets separated by Swovarski quartz crystals made with unique closures. I made those so frequently and clients just loved them! Those were fun projects but time-consuming to complete. Each one took hours to make, hand-crafted with special care. None of these ever "netted me" much money but I basically enjoyed working with the local women and creating a special remembrance for their families to pass on to their children—something special for the Moms.

It was more about the ART and gift of crafting rather than about making money.

I did so much beading this was around the time when my 20/20 vision started to fail slightly. At first I needed 150's, over the counter eyeglasses. Nothing drastic but it made a huge difference. While beading, I also starting reading the smallest, little spreadsheets for my job, something many sales managers are required to do to manage their business portfolio. I had worked on financial budgets for years but this time around, the amount of numbers crammed into one financial spreadsheet which 'fit to a page' made my eyes go bonkers, and now I needed these eyeglasses daily. I am thankful, even to this day, that my eyesight has not gotten any worse, but I know now it had a lot to do with the nighttime beading, and the excel spreadsheets—I'd never admit this to getting older! If the 150's are a requirement nowadays it doesn't stop me from pursuing my dreams with baubles or any new interests.

****

At this store in Chester, I rented a large space for almost seven years. It was a great store whereby I would stock, manage the inventory, display, price, and promote my holiday merchandise.

This company handled all the sales. A nice collaboration and they just took a cut (percentage of sales) of what was sold. It was well worth it and someone was always there to answer questions about my products. I purchased jewelry displays and officially launched Beaded Baubles, LLC when I joined this Chester retail company—it was a fun time, and it was shortly after 9/11 when we had moved to New Jersey from Rhode Island when I put this all into PLAY.

So the change was welcome while I was job hunting and going thru a career transition as well. The market had dropped so I got creative. Looking back, I am proud of myself and my first business accomplishments. Maybe I should have kept at it and just ignored the complaints I heard at home about beading. I did let my spouse's negative influence wear on me. After all, I was providing for my family, never missed a beat at home or at work, and I enjoyed what I was doing—nothing was ever jeopardized except my sleep. But somehow I was not confident enough in my marriage to stand up the way I do now and so I slowly learned to become confident as a women, and to do what made me happy. That's what entrepreneur's do best. We work hard, so we can PLAY hard later, and to enjoy life to its fullest to reap the benefits for our family.

****

While I was pitching baubles to other local merchants and after these home shows I drove my jewelry collection around to various retail storefronts to see if they would be interested in displaying the line. You won't believe this, but my first large retail customer of interest became Lilly Pulitzer of New Jersey. In fact, not one store, but all three commercial retail storefronts in the state! Lilly's Glen Ridge, Summit and Bay Head, New Jersey stores all decided to sell my baubles! I was in business!! But just a few months later, Lilly's corporate headquarters had signed on a big deal to carry their own jewelry line so they could no longer represent anyone else's baubles. It was disappointing but I knew I was onto something BIG so I didn't feel bad about my short-term experience. In fact, it was exhilarating and reconfirming to know that I did a good job and this was my first corporate success story in this new industry.

A note about Lilly Pulitzer . . . , she was a fashion icon and recently died at the age of 81 years old in 2013. Her story was that "her clothing was accessible to most, but really wearable only by the few who were so rich that they could afford to have bad taste,' states Thom Forbes of Mediapost.com (April 28, 2013). "A mini-dress of green peacocks dancing with merry seashells is not just for anyone. As for the Camelot angle, among those who could carry it off was First Lady Jackie Kennedy . . . she wore one of Lilly's dresses! It was made from kitchen curtain material—and people went crazy. They took off like zingo. Everybody loved them, and I went into the dress business," states Pulitzer and co-author Jay Mulvaney.

What an inspiration Lilly Pulitzer. A great success story of a woman entrepreneur from the early fashion years that lasted generation to generation and still has its following!

My daughter and I certainly wore many of the Lilly styles and used to visit her retail stores in Nantucket, the Vineyard and then in New Jersey after we moved there. It was always our thing growing up in Grosse Pointe to wear the blue and yellow, pink and green, or pink and yellow, various colored brands of Lilly. We saw them moving from the Midwest to the Northeast to the New England states, I saw Lilly as an established brand all over the U.S.

http://www.mediapost.com/publications/article/197528/ lilly-pulitzer-81-fashion-designer-by-accident. html?edition=58561#axzz2bcqmDunF

* * *

I'd like to thank my dear friend and colleague from Massachusetts, Gwyn Thakur, who creatively helped me coin the business name, **Beaded Baubles, LLC** She was a great sounding board and understood my business initiatives. After I launched my LLC in 2000, each year I would buy and sell about ten grand worth of merchandise and break even. It took a few years to get it going and to get out of the *red* but it didn't take long.

©Marty Bucella   www.martybucella.com

"Hire someone with Photoshop experience to
make these sales figures look better."

It was a small business, fun yet exhausting. I traveled to the NYC Accessory Show and would buy in large quantities once I learned the ropes and it was addictive! It was my therapy for a broken marriage that no one knew about and someday when the kids were older, I would fix it and tell them. I just didn't have that figured out yet so I kept on 'beading'. Colorful beautiful bold baubles. Bold colors which brought me joy.

****

At the NYC Accessory Shows I could venture off and buy other products with my sales and distribution license including accessories such as purses, totes, flip/flops, scarves . . . I diversified my Beaded Baubles product offering a bit to entice customers with my jewelry line at home shows with a flare of Jean's style but never lost sight of my main baubles product line. I just mixed it up to offer a diverse set of stylish offerings to compliment my jewelry and clients loved it, and of course, I did too! I always kept something for me that I made and wore it to show it off!

About twice a month on a Saturday mornings, I would get up and spend from 8:00 am to noon restocking my point of purchase displays to straighten up the merchandise on the shelves. For the holidays, I would decorate the shelves, as the other vendors would do, with holiday decorations and entice customers to drop by my display and offer special promotions. It gave me an opportunity to see what the retail world was like while launching my own business without having all the responsibility (and headache) of owning your own storefront. While I did not own the operations at this store, I simply managed my piece of that display and that was enough for me at that time. It was very fulfilling and it made me very happy.

In July, 2007, about seven years later, I decided to take a break, close down the retail store, and have a final sale.

Then, about 30 days later, ironically, I was diagnosed with the '**BIG C**'—breast cancer. One might say, in hindsight, it was meant to be that I took care of closing this business the previous month because once I closed shop my world turned upside down after I folded **Beaded Baubles, LLC** and stepped into my new world of breast cancer. Somehow I felt I was sent a sign. I always believed that it was fate driving my life forward – from the time becoming a young widow, even now, making change happen in my new world as an entrepreneur.

So I put Breast Cancer into PLAY with advertising, marketing and my new world today of apparel and my first book '*BLISS!*' was just beginning, as a new entrepreneur. This really was not planned but it took my mind off my illness and gave me solutions to think about – therapy to write instead of turning to other things like drugs and alcohol to heal a failing marriage and inspiration to write and move on with my life, and then to get creative with the apparel collection. I just figured all that out and although I discuss my new initiatives a little later in this book, this is one of my dreams I am living today. It's been a long road to haul but one that is fulfilling and enjoyable, with no one to judge me to for doing what I enjoy the most. Giving back to causes that mean so much to me in which I am passionate about.

At that same time I closed shop I also had begun my divorce proceedings which initially were put on hold when first diagnosed with breast cancer, so I had a lot going on back then. I decided to give my spouse a second chance, with hopes he would support me through my breast cancer journey, but once I became strong and well enough to make smart decisions, I had to re- file, it just did not work out and wasn't meant to be. He wasn't at my side through thick and thin and that was the last straw. My happiness in the marriage was short-lived. There was no more beading for therapy. I became confident with my final decision and my beautiful children gave me the strength and resilience to proceed. The divorce and custody battle were beyond amicable, but that's very common for most couples as I learned with young children.

Finally, the pieces fell into place as it were and the shop closed just in the nick of time when diagnosed with breast cancer. Just in time for me to take care of myself and my wonderful children. As you will read in **BLISS!** I actually divorced for LOVE. Sometimes when we learn *'you can't change one's behavior unless they are willing to change it themselves'*, the lightbulb went off and that's when my sales savviness went into PLAY and I got smart. I realized if my spouse truly loved his kids he would do something to help himself and so he did. You see, I left for love. I have no regrets and forced him to grow up and change his behavior by divorcing. Sounds crazy right? Well not after 15 years of trying to "fix it". People "can" change, if they want to they will. Perhaps I didn't mean enough to him to make things work with us and I'm okay with that now. I've learned a lot about life, myself and relationships that I know will take me to the next step in my journey and that's what's important – that I learned something from this too. I divorced and fought for primary custody to protect my children and will never have any regrets and am happy that I now I can **LIVE My Dreams**. I was held back, threatened and not confident in my personal life.

I am living the life I should have been living a long time ago. I am proud of my life and family – personal and professional accomplishments and that's what living your dreams is all about. Being happy with your decisions, accountable and owning up to your choices.

It was a difficult time all around and a hard, bold decision to make but I made it just the same. The work wasn't worth the time and effort unless I moved the baubles business to the next phase which would have required a great deal of overnight travel at industry trade shows and retail events. It would have taken a long-time and commitment to turn this so-called hobby into a real profitable business. As I discussed, my homefront was my main priority and I could not invest this time and energy then so my dreams were put on hold.

For now, I remembered what I learned and knew how to launch and to make smart business decisions. For now, I had to make another business decision—do it myself, hire someone to do it for me, sell the business, find a manufacturer - yes, there were many options, but with my marital life winding down, I was walking in unchartered territory. Family priorities took place over professional and then my health became my focus and priority along with my kids.

****

I chose to table my dreams and focus on my family's needs and those of children. I would eventually get back to Living My Dreams—I just didn't know when. That is exactly what I did. Again, no regrets. I cumulated a basement full of colorful and creative inventory that would be used as future birthday and holiday gifts. I donated thousands of dollars of merchandise to a Susan G. Komen Pink Tie Ball auction for their Red Rose Gala fundraiser one year. I received tax deductions, and determined "what's next" in my world of entrepreneurism while starting a new chapter in life about learning to fight breast cancer.

I knew many friends and individuals appreciated the labor of love that went into my work when they received one of my personal crafts. I really enjoyed making jewelry—it was a personal and rewarding hobby especially when my clients were pleased with my work.

JEAN CRISS MEDIA

Chapter Three

MEDIA AGENCY
(Business Phase)

The next three weeks were spent organizing my jewelry inventory in the basement, closing the business, bank accounts and related financial matters. I then began to look forward to our first annual family reunion, a vacation we were planning in Bay Harbor, Michigan that August, 2007. My entire family traveled there and we were having a good time in the sun and swimming in the pool and sightseeing. That morning, after listening to Robin Roberts of ABC Good Morning America announce her diagnosis with breast cancer to the world on National News, I then received my cell phone call while by the poolside with the shocking news that my breast MRI was positive, both sides. I later learned when I returned home, and was re-evaluated with further testing, that this was my breast cancer (bi-lateral) diagnosis phone call.

In the end, with this heavy news, I felt relieved that just a mere 3-4 weeks prior, it was almost fate, that I had recently folded one of my first dreams of my life, the launch of **Beaded Baubles, LLC**.

And I saw my life change, at the drop of a pin.

I thought to myself, God has a funny way of working with us— follow his path and he will guide you to your next venture, and someday, that will include good health and wellness. So I just closed my eyes and prayed for that.

* * *

I used the same approach after I launched Jean Criss Media, LLC—I had always wanted to launch my own media business after working in the corporate world for twenty some years and now was the chance to do just that. I had tried it once before but the day I was to quit work and resign, my deal fell thru—what timing back then, I thought to myself. It wasn't meant to be. What I had learned in the process, was how to get things going—how to set up a business, an ad agency in the form of an LLC. I had thought through what was required to get a business started out the gate so when I tried it again, it wasn't as foreign as you would have thought, but still just as challenging.

© Randy Glasbergen
glasbergen.com

"I always give 110% to my job —
40% on Monday, 30% on Tuesday, 20% on
Wednesday, 15% on Thursday and 5% on Friday."

One day I had an opportunity to start an advertising agency for three (3) key clients who previously asked me to represent them. In total, their business represented well over $8M in net ad sales day one. The business would offer media strategy, ad planning and buying, and measurement, that sort of marketing program for F500 and local businesses, but unfortunately, that day never happened. That is just how volatile the advertising business is. One day you can have clients lined up, and the very next day, they can be gone that fast. A deal is not a deal until a contract is in hand – well even though I learned this early on in my sales career, sometimes, even the contract was meaningless because large corporations can shift plans at any time and that is exactly what happened. Ironically, it had a lot to do with corporate restructuring and new board decisions and I just could not take it as personal. The first client was a large regional Hispanic insurance client who had asked me to represent his company, however, his Board of Trustees chose a respected board member in lieu of me. They never even heard my pitch that day, unfortunately after all my hard work. I spent months preparing for that "pitch" and my meeting never took place.

The second client was a F500 national window manufacturer that had a recent corporate restructuring and moved their corporate offices along with ad budgets back to their headquarters, out of state. A good portion of their local field sales offices national ad budget was reallocated so there went another couple million dollars in ad spending.

The last, third launch client was still around but insufficient funding to carry my business forward so I chose to do nothing with it. That was my short- stint at a mini-launch, if you will, in the ad agency business.

I knew how to create the LLC and had the papers ready to fax to the State office that day. I had my resignation letter ready for my employer but did not submit it. I wrote my clients and colleagues a farewell note and never sent those either since I never left the office that day. It was just an ordinary day in the corporate workplace in which I attended traditional sales and marketing meetings like any other normal workdays (and so, I kept on dreaming)! All in all, it worked out for the best at that time.

I got the official "farewell" from my employer, years later, a mere two weeks before the big NBC acquisition in the cable and broadcast TV industry, back in December 2010. So then, I decided I would attempt this media agency launch one more time and give it my "all". Although I continued to job search for full-time employment in the corporate world simultaneously, unsure if the self-employment gig would stick, I multi-tasked as many new entrepreneurs do. I had hefty bills to pay and a family to support so being practical was top of mind.

"Don't be silly. I didn't ask you here to fire you. If I wanted to do that, I'd text you."

"Linda, is it proper etiquette to announce layoffs via a Tweet?"

In January 2011, I re-filed with the State of New Jersey, and launched **Jean Criss Media, LLC**. Within weeks, I had business cards, a logo, the official papers filed, and a website under development for a creative media services agency. I wasn't sure what I would be doing exactly nor whom my clients were but I knew I was determined to succeed—whether being self-employed or back in the corporate world, I was always a multi- tasking business woman so I launched both campaigns at once. I was assertive and did the job search while planning the launch of my new business simultaneously. Some may think, 'how can you focus and do both that well?' To me, it was the same as launching multiple products as an entrepreneur, looking back. If you are determined to succeed, you set your mind at it and can make anything happen!

Believe that no matter how well you do something, you can always do it better. And chances are you will! Make change happen and believe in your dreams. These are my beliefs!

©Marty Bucella   www.martybucella.com

"Your stolen identity has shown up on eBay.
Do you want to bid on it?"

It was exciting to see it all come into PLAY. I spent many hours designing and writing for my website. I thought the web developers simply should have done all that—but the partner I hired only handled the postings while I submitted all the content, links, images, etc. the way in which you wanted the information to appear online. WOW! That was a lot of work! I didn't necessarily agree with that strategy especially after I had agreed to pay someone very high fees for web services. But I was already late in getting my website up and running fast so I stuck with this particular developer. It was time consuming, one conference call after another, and then, she kept insisting to train me on how to program in *WIX* and *Go Daddy.*. *Frankly,* I had better things to do with my time than to become a programmer, I thought to myself. I provided her all the necessary data upon request, from web design outline, content, and file layout. I did not want to spend my days consumed launching my business as a 'technology programmer' nor a 'software developer' even with all the new apps on the market which allowed you to 'plug 'n play' while attempting to launch a start-up business. They were simply too time-consuming to learn and I could not afford that time. After all, I needed time to focus on the sales and marketing aspects of my new job rather than sit behind a desk and programming a newly designed website. As it was, I spent hours upon hours, finding files and writing copy to submit, much of this content which I would have thought should have come from a good web designer.

In the end, I know I chose the wrong business partner but nonetheless, I finished my work with her and although it took a very long time to launch and get it right, I learned that sometimes it's best to part ways earlier on that to try to make something stick. Once you are thrown into a project, it's best to turn away than to just keep trying to make amends to make it work. I looked within and found comparisons with what I was doing with business and in my personal life. Too much compromise was bad business, at work or at home. I got smart, on both sides of the fence.

****

In fact, here I had designed my website by hand, and had written the web content on a sheet of paper while on a return flight home from a trip out West after visiting a dear girlfriend in Southern California. I then converted this information onto an excel spreadsheet and created tabs for each Web page. Each excel tab represented a Web page on the future Website, and all the content that should follow on each page. I thought this was a good way to structure the content for the site, and learned how to submit the information to a Web Designer. Little did I know, that I had to go deeper and submit all the links, images, photos, articles, logo's and write the detailed copy for each page at great length. OMG! Yes, I did that too!

I really wasn't sure what I was paying this woman for other than a simple outline and a template but in the end, it looked good and I guess that was all that mattered. *Well not really.*

Nowadays, those templates are pre-baked for any novice to jump start and create a new website on your own, but a few years back, the coding was customized and created from scratch. Since I did all the up-front development prep for the website, I added my name to the website as a co-designer and we published it. By the time we launched, I knew it was time for the next upgrade, and I'd be bringing my business elsewhere.

C'est la vie, as they say. That's life!

Months later, I learned my newly, designed website was developed using the wrong software platform and was incompatible on most smart phones after I launched in the Summer of 2011. By then, new smart devices were coming to market so frequent— fast and furry. Within six months I learned my website which had launched in May 2010 was already "outdated." New tablets and smart phones were on the market using new technology which required a complete re-write in **_HTML5_**, **_Word Press_**, or another application like **_Squarespace_**. I researched and found another business to handle the next redesign. I spent too much time on the ops side of my business rather than on sales and marketing side then but that's what you learn as a new entrepreneur. You may start small and need to be the expert at many things. A one woman show at first, so to speak. The operations, development, marketing, promotions and research takes you away from the core business development of sales I learned and I had to turn this around.

Back in the Summer of 2011, this poor platform launch may have been avoided if the right code was used out the gate. I wasn't familiar with all the proper questions to ask, not knowing the development side of the business. It's just one of those things you learn as you go as a new entrepreneur, which cost me time and money.

One of the things you will find with the launch of your business is you need to be very hands on, with all aspects of the business. You often learn as you go, or *Grow as you Go* – as they say, but that education is invaluable. Once you get that type of experience, you can take it anywhere and by having that, you can speak in front of your customer's with affirmation and confidence which makes all the difference between selling your product or service so much easier.

****

I was now beyond the Mini-Launch phase of my creative media services business and ready to outline and describe what the business should look like and entail in detail now.

However, while designing this site, I sent multiple resumes to the corporate world in search of a digital media job of interest or contract work. It was that multi-tasking thing I mentioned earlier that I kept up with. Just like beading at night.

I would talk to recruiters, search the web, conduct phone and do **_Skype_** interviews, make it to the top 1st or 2nd, or 2nd or 3rd tier candidates at boutique or small firms of interest, but never landed the jobs. I heard you don't have enough financial experience, marketing experience in this particular area, you are over-qualified in sales and we need to pay less, we need someone with twice as much digital media experience (even though those products were not on the market longer than they were asking), and silly things like that. While I attempted to make ends meet on the home front and kept my personal business close to the vest, I launched my new website. I probably would have folded shop if a great corporate offer was the right one. I was now a single Mom with two kids to support, no alimony and child support wasn't enough to feed a small fish tank, let alone two growing children. I had to get aggressive so dual job searching was my gig and I kept at it.

I landed a few contract jobs and enjoyed that. While I built my business, for those clients that didn't pay up and on time, I would drop them like a dime. If they didn't appreciate and value my work, then I chose not to continue to do business with them. It was plain and simple. I was not some big corporate powerhouse carrying 120 day old receivables as in the corporate world. It was my prerogative since I was now the boss. It gave me a sense of appreciation for my work and empowerment. I didn't have to do business with anyone that did not respect my work ethics or follow thru on our agreed upon Scope of Work Agreement. So as I pushed thru to succeed, I networked a lot, kept at it, attended numerous women's entrepreneur meetings and made the most of my time, as most struggling entrepreneurs do.

At some point though I hit a wall just about 8-12 months into it and decided I had to focus on one or the other career choices. In order to make my own business succeed, I had to give up on the corporate world idea and invest in my business both time and money in order for one to succeed. So that's what I did.

I plunged forward and first laid out the pros and cons of both and clearly decided I was ready for entrepreneurship full-time! I left the concept of "corporate" behind after spending over 25 years there, I felt truly accomplished in what I was doing all along. I was relieved and started getting more and more creative and my business ideas started to flourish. I was exhilarated and full of creative ideas every day and let loose. No one was previously holding me back but my own pride.

What you see today is the development of numerous innovations I created within a short window based on my determination to succeed. I couldn't have done this without looking at my children's faces each and every day. They must have wondered "what is Mom up to in that office?" After all, I left the hectic paying corporate world, long 12-14 hour days, with the long-commute to be closer to home. But now I'm still working crazy long days and in fact, on many days, longer hours but I realize the time and investment will pay off. They agreed they **did** love having Mom at home . . . . more home cooked meals, time to attend their after school activities, take them "to and fro" their social activities (even though the chauffeuring has become challenging with their youthful teen years). I wasn't bringing in the bacon so to speak so cutting into my day job was eating at my time. I had to cut corners around the house which they noticed and I tried to maximize my time and our household expenses like any solo- preneur would do. I worked all hours of the day and night, and invested in myself and my business. I stopped shopping, something I enjoyed immensely but really didn't need the wardrobe anymore and missed my "Bloomie" gals. The light in my home office was on at least 16-18 hours/day—Yes, I was working hard and diligently to succeed.

©Marty Bucella   www.martybucella.com

"We no longer look at résumés. We go straight to your Facebook page."

This mini-launch became the true testament of my skills set and confidence to move forward. ***Ladies Who Launch,*** a national women's entrepreneur organization, and the first one that I joined in NYC, connected me to many women when I got started. In fact, I took my first 'Incubator Training Course' with them, attended various Press Relations meetings, and other NYC events with other female entrepreneurs—more on that shortly. ***B.I.G*** was one local women's organization which really stated the way I felt about myself . . . to ***Believe, Inspire, and Grow*** as an entrepreneur. Although I felt that this organization was more intended for Mom's transitioning from the home back into the workforce, I took out of it what I could by simply networking with other women entrepreneurs— it had more of the basic 101 classes and I progressed much further along in my business planning than what I learned my two years there. Then, there were many other women's leadership and business organizations which I joined throughout the NYC area which I will discuss later in this book about the impact these women made and how I leveraged these organizations with my best practices to succeed in business.

© Randy Glasbergen
www.glasbergen.com

"I have a hard time finding a balance between work and work."

My mini-launch was off to a good start, as they say, and "Life is good".

Life is good.

"The important thing is not being afraid to take a chance. Remember, the greatest failure is to not try. Once you find something you love to do, be the best at doing it."

-*Debbi Fields*

Chapter Four

INCUBATOR
(Platform & Strategy)

At that same time, I focused on my new redesign website and began to craft new enhancements to build my business in many directions.

By now, **Jean Criss Media, LLC** was formed and well on its way, about 18 months later. I had a handful of clients and I was multi-tasking as many new entrepreneurs do—working hard, smart, and fast. Trying to make ends meet and also still looking for that big break—whether it is a big retainer, contract, or a corporate job I really didn't want to go back to the corporate world as I was really enjoying the self-employment gig. However, I was a single Mom with two teens and had **BIG** bills to pay. No alimony nor unemployment and with only a few pennies in child support, which basically paid for milk and bread, it was all up to me to be the creative one and head of household (again).

So what was new with that? Nothing at all.

"By not looking for a job, I'm opening a spot
for another job seeker, so in fact, I'm
really a job creator."

I was used to being the primary bread winner for 15 years in my second marriage. I just had to believe in myself. I would not let anyone cut me down. Focus on all the positive things in life and positive people. Walk away from all negative things and people. 'Unfriend or De-friend Your Fears' as the saying goes. If they did not believe in me, I choose not to give them attention and they were basically 'short lived' on my schedule. I learned that friends can be callous and jealous, even with things you may <u>not</u> have, but when they see that you are determined to succeed and have the desire to make things happen, some like to stand in your way.

"It's worse than being fired. I'm unfriending you."

DE-FRIEND
YOUR FEARS.

Karen Salmansohn
best selling author of
The Bounce Back Book

On a more positive note, I liked being called a 'mover and shaker' especially by my recent Entertainment Attorney, and I suppose, he is right. I always make things happen in my life and would not have it any other way for me and my children. We deserve happiness and success. BLISS!— as I write. We had experienced enough drama in our lives and I wanted personal success so that we could reap the rewards of a good life.

"I like to begin every performance review with a compliment. Boy, I look good today!"

My work life was no longer about driving corporate perks, assessing performance reviews or team building. It was about sustainable products and solutions for my clients, creative media and marketing programs that delivered high-end results and innovative media services which offer new ways to go to market.

"It's been a tough quarter, so in lieu of bonuses, you'll all be receiving a DVD of out-takes from our meetings."

* * *

Jean Criss Media, LLC is a creative media services agency comprised of the following offerings. . . business consulting in multi- media, integrated marketing across various product platforms and brands with emphasis in these three areas; digital media, culinary, and luxury and entertainment. At my boutique agency, we utilize best practices by combining market strategy, design expertise and common business sense; we enhance client's market visibility and potential to engage its audience effectiveness.

I personally have a passion to service the health and wellness industry and created cause-related products that are currently under development for breast cancer survivors with a new fashion line I designed I became an author by utilizing my digital media expertise and put that into PLAY with self-publishing by writing, designing and editing a three book trilogy series before bringing those to market.

I've created this new collection of products in the areas of book publishing, product and design patents for future fashion apparel, have music concepts underway, and have other product patent ideas in the works that peak my interest over the years bringing inspiration, creativity with future results to my bottom line. My agency uses the same level of creativity to bring inspiration and creativity to achieve your business goals. JC Media's platform of products and media services was created in less than 18 months initially which allowed me to showcase a portfolio of media services in the marketplace and extend new products to future clientele. I thrive on new ideas and putting them into PLAY for my clients.

My current media portfolio of services includes: Business Consulting, Digital Media and Social Media, Television Advertising & Production, Public Relations, Print Publishing and Advertising, Festivals and Event Productions, Corporate Sponsorship Sales, Media Strategy and Buying, Brand Development, Radio and Outdoor, and other creative productions and innovative solutions. Learn more about them at JeanCrissMedia.com.

An unparalled approach to customer first by engaging the customer to **DISCUSS** their needs, **CREATE** a platform of solutions, **COLLABORATE** on agreed upon direction and strategy, **MEASURE** with actionable next steps, **INVOLVE** and participate at all levels of client and customer organization, and **PROMOTE** to B2C and/or B2B audiences.

* * *

I had joined a five-week intense incubator course for women entrepreneurs. I was new to this organization but wasn't there to make friends necessarily, although I did, and lasting ones too.

Moreover, I was there to learn and grow, and network, as a newly founded entrepreneur—to grow and establish myself in a new world surrounded by intriguing and inspiring women, and to figure out my next move in business.

The class consisted of a small group—eight women. We became close friends—launched and lunched together after our half-day intensive class(es). A jewelry designer; a make-up artist who later became a social media consultant (go figure!); a bio-physicist who was becoming a life-coach/consultant in her technology field—amazing; another life coach—a Mom returning to the workforce as a life coach; an art director in the NYC theatre; and me—a media/technologist with too many ideas!

Our class leader had a Master's in positive psychology, or happiness as she stated, from UPenn.

She was an amazing woman and we are still close friends today. She also launched a new biz while coaching others too. She showed us the ropes and I learned that all my 'crazy ideas' were not so crazy after all!

"I can live with you not wanting to push the
envelope, but your refusal to think
outside the box..."

She inspired us and taught me not only about 'how to launch my business' but gave me the self-confidence and direction I needed for my strategy, planning and taught me how to take a break too. She would say, 'Jean, if you need to rest and take a nap—just do that!' I would laugh and say, 'what?! Are you crazy? Who has time for a nap?! **I don't nap!** I just keep going like the energizer bunny! And we would laugh!' But she gave me good advice. One thing about being an entrepreneur is that you learn how to be better at time management. It's okay to have some downtime—to refresh the mind, body and soul. Just when you think you had mastered it in the corporate world, you need to do a better job out on your own. I had to juggle the home office gig, being the chauffeur with my kids, as I no longer could afford to employ a nanny or home sitter (the kids were not babies anymore), and had to work my business around their school day and my parenting/custody schedule, and my commutes to and from the city (New York). It got a little crazy but I kind of got used to it. It required I worked many evenings and attended many events. It was frustrating at times but well worth the personal reward to spend more time with my family which I never had before. It required a lot of coordination on my part. The kids were happy and independent and that was important to me. I was the one who had to figure it out, most of all!

At least I was cooking for my kids, more often than before while in the corporate world, healthy fresh cooked meals and they liked that. Some mornings I would prepare their dinner by 8 am before I left for the city and my daughter would just need to turn the stove or oven on—simple things so at least I knew they got a home-cooked meal. Now I realized I needed to do more for myself. It was time to do things for "me" and continue to care for my family and less for the corporate world. It felt good and right.

I attended soccer games, track meets, and other school activities that previously—was faux pas if I had to leave a corporate meeting early as my former boss/employer didn't like. It was disappointing to the kids. Times you never forget and regret—some managers were not all that understanding or compassionate. I recalled I had days of resentment while working for corporate employers while being required to attend company functions or meetings, always being on their clock, not having independence in the workforce. Some managers were just so damn demanding and unforgiving! I don't think all companies operate this way but some "manager's" do. My new life gives me the freedom to do as I please and I began to see smiles ☺ on my kids' faces and no one could replace that! Not a pay check, not a sales award or a '**team**' plaque, or an excellence leadership award or performance review!

During these incubator classes, we would all gather around with a chair and form a circle. One at a time, we would update one another on our projects, with a time limit—love that! Always structured meetings, and to the point. Concise and direct!

We had homework for ourselves too and for each other. Yes, we had to write and think about each other's businesses which made it exciting to give one another ideas about how to help other grow their business and inspire our colleagues. It got emotional for some of us. If it "hit home", we just supported one another. What mattered most was that we were there for one another, like sisters—our incubator sisterhood. It was a great learning experience.

If you were late to the meetings in NYC—you snooze, you lose! We started without you. Not an easy thing with all the commuting for everyone but we had a schedule to stick too and I loved that too. We were there to crunch! Afterall, my commute was 1.5 – 2 hours from NJ each way many days and if I could get there on time, the locals should be able to get there too.

We all were pursuing our dreams! Soon to be living them—that is what we had to remind ourselves—so stay focused and soon we would *LIVE Our Dreams* and that's when I got the idea for this new story.

I began to document what I was doing and how I was planning my next steps with my entrance into the world as a media-preneur.

The definition of Incubator defined by the *Ladies Who Launch* organization Incubator course was defined as follows; Ideas need support and action in order to grow and thrive. The Incubator was designed to give you and your ideas a perfect "growth" environment. Its equal parts focus group, resource-sharing space, and supportive community, and then another intangible part that you can't really imagine until you experience it. The group consists of 10 or so other resourceful, inspiring women who help one another take their projects, businesses, or ideas to a new place. One night a week for four weeks (or mornings, depending on the schedule), under the leadership of a trained *Ladies Who Launch* facilitator, met with our group, completed "homework" for ourselves and for each other, and found an uncommon bond that exists between women traveling down their own path.

When the Incubator Intensive ends, we were invited to join our Incubator Ongoing program; a year-long membership (price varies per market) that encompasses many of the same benefits you find within your Incubator, but with 100 times the resources and access. Among the benefits:

8-12 meetings per year with amazing speakers (women who have launched hugely successful businesses or have skills to share about launching a business).

• Discounts to our BYOB (Be Your Own Boss) events

• PR opportunities not available to non-members

• Credits for free advertising on our site

The Incubator is for any woman, with any business or any project. Whether you feel "stuck" and need to get out of a rut, have hit a plateau in your business, or just want to figure out what's next, the Incubator increases momentum and clarifies your vision. The Ongoing Incubator gives you daily, weekly, and monthly doses of education, opportunity, and inspiration . . . and so much more. www.ladieswholaunch.com. This was part of the key to my success and I thrived on these meetings!

* * *

We built our pyramids. Not the 'ACME' model or any other pyramid scheme on the market you might be thinking about rather our real own creative strategies. This was our foundation for success! We created a personal map about our credentials, functional benefits, emotional benefits, values, personality, target audience insight, positioning, and our imperative—an 8-layer cake filled with yummy definitions to our future success. Your launch / self-map.

My Imperative

My Positioning

My Target Audience Insights

My Personality

My Values

My Emotional Benefits

My Functional Benefits

My Credentials

My Imperative: To help clients succeed in unique and creative ways. Win/win, customer first.

My Positioning: A collaboration of client's visions combined with my media and technology expertise put to work (best practices).

My Target Audience Insights: Multiple disciplines, target markets, demographics, geo-marketing and audience segmentations depending upon budget P&L. Focused business categories: Experiential— technology/digital, auto, etc. Luxe—includes spa, fashion, entertainment, etc. Culinary—food, wine, spirits.

My Personality: Unique and authentic, savvy selling power. Strong marketing, sales, leadership, general business management, communication skills and am passionate, assertive, self-motivated, dedicated/serious, and compassionate driver.

My Values: High-level customer satisfaction, out-of-box solutions, high- integrity and turnaround.

My Emotional Benefits: 1on1, confident, boutique agency, payoff, customer 1st strategy, client needs are met and important.

My Functional Benefits: Ad strategy, buys, placements, market impacts and inherent change on one's business. Use numerous mediums and partners to accomplish client goals—mediums: cable & broadcast TV, print, digital and social media, Internet/ Web, radio, video, marketing collateral, etc.

My Credentials: Successful media and tech career, 24 yrs, yielding over $100M net sales ($70M multi-media; $30M volume corp. sales). Recently left prestigious corp. world to spread wings and become entrepreneur, utilize best practices in biz by creating multi-media solutions beyond traditional advertising solutions.

Jean Criss Media favorite quote: '*A goal is simply a dream with a deadline*'.

So start with a blank pyramid and start building your plan! I always refer to my "8-layer cake" and indulge in some too! Choc-o-late if I get a preference! Healthy mind, healthy body and spirit!

Here are other pyramids which you might find useful to your planning or be familiar with including Maslow's Heirarchy of Needs which I found interesting in comparison to various business pyramids and models.

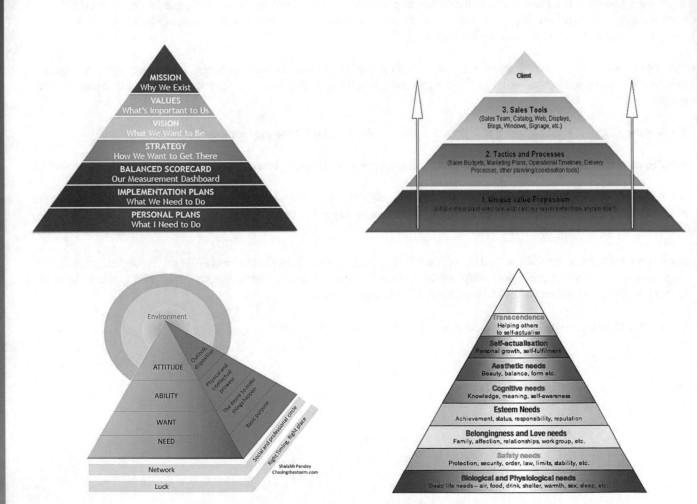

Thank you ***Ladies Who Launch.com***, specifically to Victoria Colligan, Founder, for the opportunity and my two Executive Directors, Stella Grizont and Karla Lighthouse. About a year later, I was asked to run the New Jersey franchise by these women leader's which intended to split the NYC/NJ chapters but I honestly did not want to invest in their organization as opposed to investing in mine. My dream of making my wish come true was sitting in front of me and I needed to follow my path and pursue that grid that I had just created. I realized their offer wasn't the direction I aspired to pursue so I declined this thrilling opportunity, and it made me realize I was good at what I was doing, and just reconfirmed I needed to focus more on that and put more emphasis into my own pyramid to ensure I would succeed.

I also learned from Founder, Victoria Colligan, that it is helpful to have a broader understanding of what it means to be 'happy'. "Positive psychology experts have identified a happiness framework that contains three distinct kinds of happiness. In a nutshell they are:

1. Pleasure (instant gratification, quick stimuli happiness like food, sex, shopping or wine)
2. Passion (being in the "flow" of an activity in which you barely notice the passage of time like running, writing, certain work modes or creativity / building mindsets), and
3. Purpose (feeling connected to a higher sense of why you are here and what you are meant to do or achieve)."

For me, that sense of happiness resides in identifying the wherewithal of the moment—the who you are with, where you strive to go or be, who you want to be or be with, and why you want to be there. 'When love whispers, the heart listens' I once read. Continually evaluate your emotions and actions to reach your utmost potential, I told myself!

Victoria rephrased her eight-year old daughter's questions . . .

Are you the person you want to be now?
Are you dreaming the dream?
Launching the dream?
Living the dream?
Are you happy?

I ask myself that and my answer is YES—what's yours? Thanks Victoria and LWL!

* * *

Before I continue on, I'd like to share with you a good article about other Incubator programs that you may find useful. Published in ***Young Entreprenur.com***©, Neil Parmar, Contributor, explains how '***Startup Incubators and Accelerators Go Virtual with Limited Success,***' *August 14, 2013.*

There's been an explosion of startup incubators and accelerators in recent years. But not all of them will require you to squeeze into a shared office in Silicon Valley, the Big Apple or another major metropolis. Some of them are based, at least in part, online.

*In Australia, startups under the Melbourne Accelerator Program are taking part in a new initiative where founders will receive mentorship through the **GetViable®**, a company that launched earlier this year to provide digital tools and communication resources to help entrepreneurs grow their business. Then there's "Alice," the codename of a new web-based* *project that's set for release in October and comes from **Seeqnce®**, a startup accelerator based in Lebanon. There are few public details about Alice, though the project is designed to **scale Seeqnce's®** acceleration model so that it can serve "tens of thousands" of ventures across Europe, the Middle East and Africa.*

While there' obvious interest in online incubators and accelerators, the question is do they work? Some entrepreneurs—and even execs at incubator's—who've considered or tested these kinds of virtual environments, aren't so sure.

*Svetlana Dotsenko (right), 25, sees online incubators as a way for entrepreneurs to grow their network and secure additional investment funds. The CEO of Project Lever, a consultancy, helped implement virtual components of the **Healthbox®** accelerator program in Boston last year.*

Credit: Harvard Graduate School of Education (Education Innovation Pitch Competition)

Related: Ahoy! A Look at Startup Incubators and Excursions for Globetrotting Entrepreneurs. The challenge with relying on these kinds of services is that there can be technical glitches or quality issues with streaming. "Its technology: Sometimes it's really good, sometimes it's really bad," says Zack Miller, the 29-year-old managing director behind Hatch, a Norfolk, Virginia-based incubator that harnesses online communication tools between its members and mentors.

Some incubators and accelerators have found that virtual communication falls drastically short in comparison to face-to-face interactions. The Founder Institute, an early-stage startup accelerator in Silicon Valley, launched four years ago with the vision of starting 1,000 companies each year. It turned to the web to help broadcast its educational offerings to a wider audience, including roughly half of its original pool of participants. Yet of the 34 companies that graduated during the Founder Institute's first semester, only one from the online subgroup went on to generate substantial revenues. The remainder—worth around $1 billion today, the Founder Institute estimates—had each of their founders attend the accelerator in person.

"The social pressure gets people building their business at a faster pace," says Adeo Ressi, the institute's founder.

While the Founder Institute discontinued the virtual arm of its accelerator program after its initial pilot, it ran subsequent tests with online education— in 2010 and 2012—by providing digital videos of established business founders, among other features. Still, surveys found minimal improvements in satisfaction among treps who participated online, even though they were exposed to the exact same programming as peers who joined in person.

Related: Start-Up Chile: See Why Many Americans are Itching to Enter This Early-Stage Accelerator "You can't be an armchair person and launch a business—you have to dig your fingers into the mud," says Ressi, whose institute has helped launch more than 880 companies to date. "I'm not ruling it out, and I want to try more tests over time, but the data is very conclusive right now: Virtual incubation does not work."

Streaming technology can be hit or miss in terms of quality, says Zack Miller, 29, the managing directo of Hatch incubator. But he notes online communication can help link far-flung startups to helpful mentors. | Image Credit: Eyecaptures

*Still, advocates of online programs point to benefits like lower costs and world-wide access thanks to Skype and Google Hangouts. Programs will, for instance, share video-case studies of mentors via **Dropbox®** or they'll go through multiple edits of marketing materials tracked through a Facebook Group.*

*For others, online incubators help make a wider array of connections, which can in turn secure more investments and grow a business faster, says Svetlana Dotsenko, the 25-year-old CEO behind Project Lever, a consultancy that helped manage the online components of the **Healthbox** accelerator program when it debuted in Boston last year. "Even though it can help people connect with a mentor, it obviously can't replace in-person interaction," she says.*

*Related: How One Young Entrepreneur Wants to Transform the Great Outdoors with '**Glamping**' Dan Blacharski argues that a virtual incubator can boost a startup's marketing power and online visibility better than a brick-and-mortar one. That's what the 53-year-old trep from South Bend, Ind., found after he cycled a new venture he launched last year, Techie. com, through an online program called World Accelerator. This particular accelerator, which Blacharski says took a 10 percent equity stake in Techie.com, emphasizes the importance of starting off with a premium domain name—such as Comic. com or Accountant.com, both of which World Accelerator owns the rights to—in addition to providing growth capital and mentorship.*

*At the end of the day, none of these benefits matter without attaining buy-in from programs and participants. At this point, online incubators haven't garnered the reputation of better-known (in-house) programs such as Y **Combinator®**, says Jennifer Ping, the 30-year-old founder of Universal Insights Analytics, a Toronto-based venture that builds Info-graphic-like reporting tools and platforms for businesses such as **Pixall®**. It might be harder to foster "a relationship on a deeper personal connection," adds Ping in reference to networking through online incubators. "Face-to-face interaction is much more valuable than an online program."*

How could a virtual incubator or accelerator help your startup move to the next level?

Think about your plans and your next steps!

Other organizations that I am involved in to help me grow my business as a media-preneur are these core areas including; digital media, culinary and luxury services. ***6-Figures*** is a leading international professional business organization, ***Women's Leadership Exchange—LEXCI***—a women's leadership group, ***Ladies Who Launch***, an entrepreneurial group coaching women in business to "Dream it, Launch it, and Live it!"; at ***B.I.G.*** (Believe, Inspire, Grow) is a community based women's organization, and there are others. Professional affiliations that kept me focused in my world of digital media include *NY WIFT* (NY International Film and Television Bureau), *WICTV* (Women in Cable TV), *CAB* (Cable Advertising TV Bureau), and then networking at dozens of local chambers throughout the region.

I also am a Board member of ***The Fortnightly Club of Summit*** serving as Publicity Chair, a women's group dedicated to volunteerism, fundraising, community service and outreach. I'm a new member of the ***James Beard Foundation***, an organization dedicated to celebrate, nurture, and honor America's diverse culinary heritage through programs that educate and inspire. There are many industry affiliations and philanthropic organizations that I work closely with which empower women. You can search them here. http://jeancrissmedia.com/affiliations/.

AFFILIATIONS —Business organizations, women entrepreneur groups, breast cancer and non-profit organizations alike in which Jean Criss is passionate about. She takes time to learn, coach, network, fundraise, serve on organizational boards, or simply gives back to local communities and participates at special events which take place throughout the year. '*It's as simple as buying that cup of coffee each day when we make decisions in our life—it's worth every minute to me to give back and to raise awareness about worthy organizations. Share, learn and get involved in non-profit organizations that make a difference to you!*' Here's how you can participate in these organizations or use them as a resource guide. Give back and get involved!

Friends, Partners & Affiliations
"It takes a community to create change!" by Geena Davis.

On the next page are some wonderful groups I am proud to link to and be involved in.

Business & Women's Entrepreneur Organizations:

6-Figures (6f)
Believe Inspire Grow (B.I.G.)
Cable Ad Bureau (CAB TV)
CEO Clubs NYC
Dress for Success
Fort Nightly Club of Summit (FNC)
Geena Davis Institute on Gender in Media
    http://www.seejane.org/
Karen Salmansohn
Kris Carr
Ladies Who Launch (LWL)
New York Women in Film Television
    (NYWIFT)
OneHundredWomenMakingADifference
    (100W)
Savvy Ladies
Taybandz.org
TEDx Hoboken Women
The Three Tomatoes
Writer's Guild of America
Woman2Woman Business
Women in the World
Women's Leadership Exchange (LEXCI)
Women Owned Business Club (WOBC)
others

Breast Cancer & Non-Profit Organizations:

Alzheimer's Foundation
American Cancer Society
Americans For Responsible Solutions
Autism Speaks
Breast Cancer Research Foundation
CancerCare
Good Search (dailygood)
Gift of Life
Girls Scout's of America
Joe Torre Safe @ Home Foundation
National Breast Cancer Foundation
National Early Detection Protection
National Eating Disorder (NEDA)
National Lymphedema Network
Pink Together
Red Cross Foundation
Reeves-Reed Arboretum
Salvation Army
Stand Up 2 Cancer (SU2C)
Susan G. Komen
Tiger Lily Foundation
United Way
Women Aware, Inc.
YMCA
Young Life / Wild Lyfe
Young Women's Club of America
various local Chambers

Scan with RedLaser

Chapter Five

PLANNING & DEVELOPMENT

(Structural phase)

Have you ever heard the quote; "*out with the bad and in with the good*," well I had some structure around all this craziness and now that I had my pretty picture down on paper what was next?

I was done dealing with the negativity or those that would attempt to influence me with bad karma and preferred to surround myself with those who inspired me with positivity and creative ways. I attempted to throw out all the bad in my life and keep the good and bring in happiness! That began as the key to my success. I focused on that and this was a crucial key or piece of the platform learned in my pyramid.

However, then I felt my strategy was all over the map—working many levels and each project "*multi-taneously*". Something I knew I was good at (multi-tasking) but was certainly a challenge when you are the "do-er" for each line of the business. I decided to prioritize my list of projects based on revenue producing programs to slow it down a bit. Focus on what I could accomplish year one, then plan out year two, and beyond. What could I accomplish by December that year? Then, the next six months and so on. It made more sense to me now and seemed do-able. I did have aggressive goals and when I discussed this strategy with other women entrepreneurs I still turned their heads and overwhelmed them with all I had going on but somehow I still launched my business in the digital media marketplace, kept at that, and expanded into many new media areas including social media, public relations, video productions, TV production, and others, while writing and publishing my trilogy seriesand creating product patents and designs for a new clothing line, and tabling a few other ideas for the following year. '*WOW*', some said, but I was able to juggle a lot as one may say. In fact, I created three (3) patents—provisional and design and then the following year turned one into a utility patent and started creating prototypes for my new garment line year one. I kept creating other product patent designs and at writing and expanding my product ventures.

I spent way too many hours with legal counsel but this was all for the good as I expanded my business franchise properly. I was always interested in doing business the right way and wanted to be certain I didn't have to back track at a later date for fear of not starting off on the right foot. So I invested in myself and the business properly from the get-go. I knew it would pay off soon enough—there would be a return on investment in the near future!

At first, in a rebellious way, I followed my heart and chose not to listen to the professionals. I prioritized my schedule based on business opportunity, scope and depth of work, timelines, resources required to complete a project, and so on. I devised my own tactics to determine what was feasible year 1, 2 and 3, etc.

I may have seemingly rushed to the finish line Year 1 and completed two self-published books, and wrote half of the 3rd book by September 2012. I was a wild, crazy person—exhilarated by energy! I wasn't sleeping much—filled with happiness and it worked. True *BLISS!* I got healthy and became a five-year breast cancer survivor by January 2013! Yahoo!

I completed these first designs under a newly created **CRISSCROSS™** trademark, and decided to dedicate the first bra to my aunt who died from malignant breast cancer and the trademark name to to my deceased first husband, who died tragically in my arms post auto-accident – hence the name Criss in the brand name. We made a vow to one another from his hospital bed, minutes before he died in my arms, when he asked me to move on with my life and to let him go—so he could die peacefully. At that time, I couldn't think of it! I was hysterical when I was experiencing all this as any pending young widow would react. But somehow I agreed to keep his name forever and he told me he would watch over me, and I felt the calm. Then the doctors and nurses rushed in, and he went into cardiac arrest and had an embolism in my arms. They forced me to leave his room while they treated him. At the time, they thought it was for an upper respiratory problem, and later we learned he died of cardiac failure. It was a devastating time of my life. A young woman, filled with joy and happiness. To this day, the memories live on and will continue by creating this product line with dedication in memory to him, Al Criss, and with proceeds supporting my children's college funds and other causes which I am passionate about.

Not only am I dedicating the first bra to my Aunt Nina who died tragically from malignant breast cancer— the entire collection will be named after survivors who have made an impact in my life in some way or another helping to put an end to breast cancer forever. Another bra will be dedicated to a dear entrepreneur and friend, Christina Bloom who died this past year from re--occurring Stage 4 breast cancer. As I say, **'Don't let cancer get the BREAST of you'.**

Many women entrepreneurs congratulated me especially once the patent was approved to continue on this path to provide comfort for breast cancer survivors, 'way to go, this is the BREAST news I've heard all day!', 'know that the BREAST of us are behind you!', 'all the BREAST', and the phrases and story continued with love, hope and encouragement.

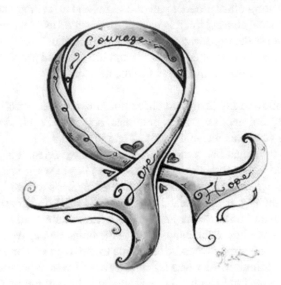

The **CRISSCROSS**™ brand was officially created and it reminded me of the old slogan 'cross your heart bras' from years ago but was nothing like that at all. I would venture into a new industry that I really knew nothing about other than beading from my bauble days (**Beaded Baubles, LLC**). My fashionista at heart took over and I put pen to paper and started designing my brands just like I had designed that website year one. What fun!

* * *

Then, came many new product inspirations—with fashion designs and patents to clothing, music CDs, spirits, digital media, television shows, gadgets, events, and other engagements for the home and business. I engulfed myself with joy to create **Jean Criss Media** enterprises and the purpose was that many of these product lines were going to support "Breast Cancer" research or go towards abused women, or various other organizations I support.

Be the kind of
woman
that when your feet
hit the floor
each morning
the devil says,
"**Oh crap,**
she's up!"

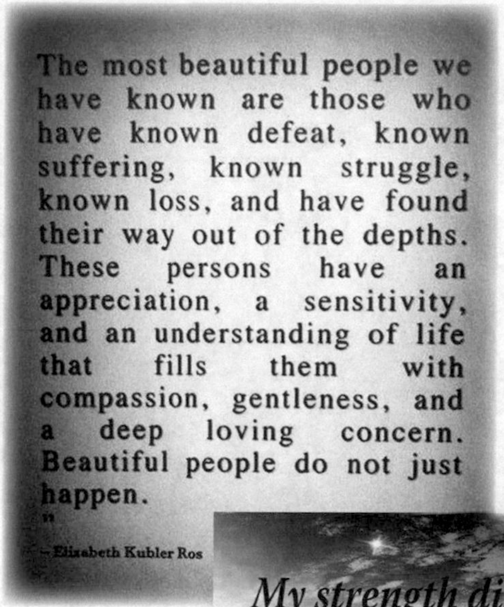

The most beautiful people we have known are those who have known defeat, known suffering, known struggle, known loss, and have found their way out of the depths. These persons have an appreciation, a sensitivity, and an understanding of life that fills them with compassion, gentleness, and a deep loving concern. Beautiful people do not just happen.
"
— Elizabeth Kubler Ros

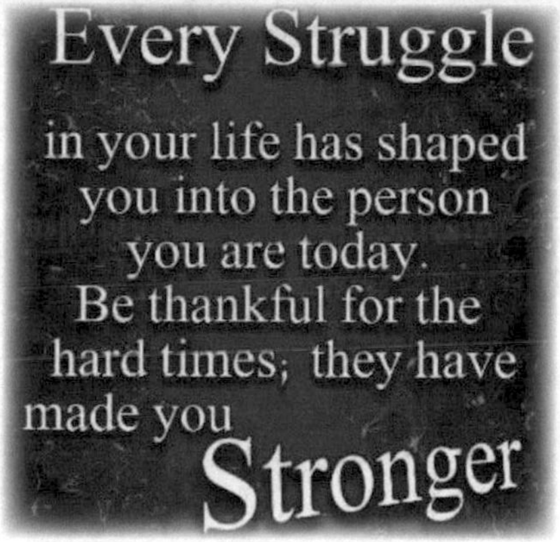

Every Struggle

in your life has shaped
you into the person
you are today.
Be thankful for the
hard times; they have
made you
Stronger

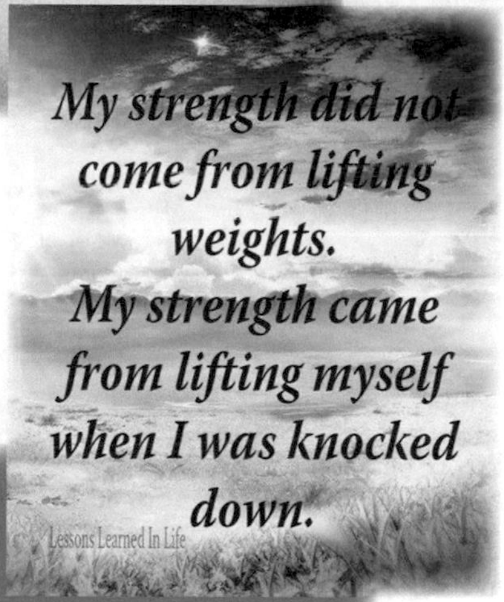

My strength did not come from lifting weights.
My strength came from lifting myself when I was knocked down.
Lessons Learned In Life

Where there is hope...
Where there is courage...

breast
There is a
SURVIVOR
cancer

Where there is strength...
Where there is determination...

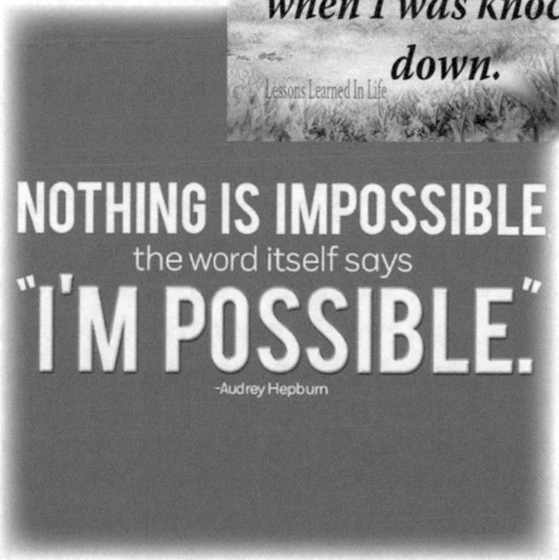

NOTHING IS IMPOSSIBLE
the word itself says
"I'M POSSIBLE."
-Audrey Hepburn

Chapter Six

LAUNCH IT!—REAL LAUNCH—LLC!

(Reality phase)

Before I could LIVE My Dreams, I had to first believe in myself. It started at the juncture of Dream Avenue and Believe Street!

So I set out to recall my most memorable and deepest thoughts and dreams—things I've always wanted to do. I made a "BIG" wish list. I made this list current. Out with the bad and in with the new! I kept all the good dreams and ideas, and jotted those down.

Then I was determined if I could take some of these ideas and turn them into a profit, I would put structure around each bullet in my plan. The launch phase could not start without knowing the 'what' and 'where' before the 'who' and why' phases though. I would answer all those pieces of the pie after I created the crust from scratch. I went to work.

Man different versions and ideas came about at first. They changed up a lot. I kept refining and redesigning my focus and areas of expertise. What I wanted to work partly because I was learning along the way and defining my strategy, or PLAY. Let's take social media as example. Local clients wanted it. They knew they needed a presence, their businesses need to get known, but they weren't really willing to pay extensively for unproven or unknown services in an untested market.

These were new and un-established technologies when I was starting out. Some clients thought social media should be a pro-bono or value- add extension to media buying. The problem with all this was the time involved in set up of these sites and the on-going maintenance. What the clients did not realize was the art required to set-up a **facebook** site, to create a fan page, to schedule weekly or monthly blogs, to learn a client's business to create promotions to engage their clients to their site with taglines or tweets that made sense. These took time and were unchartered territory to many and had value that has now been established in a short period of time. With any new media, it takes time for technology to catch on and to stick, as they say. Well my glue needed to stick out the gate and if my clients didn't have the glue, I couldn't afford to take on their craft, if you know what I mean. I said "no" to anyone who could not pay for services. Year one when I launched, I may have offered selective value—add schedules, but year two was all about being profitable. Again, if you could not pay, off you went to collections or counsel, and I went onto my next project. Plain and simple. No current or future lost wages on time-consuming collection issues or hassles. Let the experts handle all that stuff and I would work on my enterprise. I had a plan and was going to stick to my glue and strategy. My reputation preceded itself and 'I would not let anyone else's dogma bring me down'. Didn't Jobs state that?!—How right he was! A brilliant man.

Actually, to quote Steve Jobs properly it went like this; *"Your time is limited, so don't waste it living someone else's life.* **Don't be trapped by dogma—which is living with the results of other people's thinking.** *Don't let the noise of other's opinions drown out your own inner voice. Most important, have the courage to follow your heart and intuition. They somehow already know what you truly want to become. Everything else is secondary."* May 25, 2009.

Some marketing or advertising campaigns alone were so time- consuming that they did not pay off. Some say that's part of the 'pre-sales' marketing that goes with the territory. In good business, it shouldn't. Everyone knows you need to cover your costs and turn a dime and make a nickel.

A creative media services agency

I turned my numerous dreams into reality with the planning that took place before the launch. Now I'm focused on executing the strategy, 18 months later, or 2.5 years since the company launch.

JEAN CRISS MEDIA—Comprehensive creative media services for your business. Focused in experiential solutions, digital media, luxury and entertainment, fashion and apparel, culinary and spirits, publishing and non-profit, there are innovative marketing solutions in the B2C and B2B markets waiting to be revealed.

Jean also empowers women with her passionate platform of breast cancer solutions launched with *BLISS!*, **CRISSCROSS™**, and other products planned that integrate her digital media and technology expertise across publishing, fashion, entertainment, spirits and new ventures. Her goal is to continue to raise awareness and to find a cure for breast cancer. **'Don't let cancer**

get the BREAST of You!' Her motto! By utilizing her hands-on media experience and as a breast cancer survivor, she demonstrates her abilities in the non-profit world. She offers hope and encouragement for today and tomorrows breast cancer survivors providing alternative products and solutions in pursuit of happiness and to comfort their lifestyles.

EXPERIENTIAL—Jean Criss Media combines her twenty-five years of expertise in digital media and technology to provide experiential solutions, and a portfolio of production and publishing services for all your client needs.

    DIGITAL MEDIA—We start by assessing your business needs to determine the best media solutions to reach your target and demographic market audience, budget and strategic goals. Preview a snapshot of a few multi-media/digital platforms on our website; http://jeancrissmedia. com/digital/.

    PUBLISHING SERVICES—Custom publishing services for all your Print and Digital needs. Sponsorship sales, marketing, social media, press relations, and event productions. http://jeancrissmedia.com/ publishing/.

    PRODUCTION SERVICES—Custom video productions for all your business needs including short—form (:30 sec), web (up to 2 mins), long-form (up to 60 mins), corporate videos (vignettes), TV show productions (trailers, pilots, and 30 min. series as example), internet banner ads, radio jingles, music, custom compilations, and other media productions. Collaborating and creating the right media-mix to provide the highest exposure! Partnering with the industry's leading media companies, top producers and talent agencies http://jeancrissmedia. com/production/.

CULINARY: FOOD, WINE & SPIRITS—Producing Food, Wine, Spirit, and even Art and Music Festivals, collaborating with celebrity, personal & holistic Chefs and Sommeliers. We create food tastings & cooking demos at specialty gourmet kitchens or for private in-home dining experiences and offer exquisite Culinary Catering events for delectable palates, and more. Also promoting Food, Wine and Spirit TV shows with Top Celebrity Chefs & Sommelier http://jeancrissmedia. com/culinary/.

    CULINARY CUISINE SERVICES—A variety of culinary cuisine offerings including special catering events, food tastings and cooking demonstrations at gourmet kitchens and private in-home dining, Television shows about Wine & Spirits and Culinary Cuisines from these top Sommeliers and Celebrity Chefs, and other Promotional Merchandise and Programs.

LUXE—Whether you're looking for a luxurious day at the spa, a new high-end apparel garment, planning a day at your favorite hotel or simply attending a local or corporate business meeting, you will want the perks and want to know the right places to visit or how to obtain them. What's your local destination? Look no further and check out these **LUXE** venues for all your hospitality and entertainment needs.

    HOSPITALITY—**Jean Criss Media** offers the luxury and entertainment industry a variety of services involving sponsorship sales, video productions, advertising, social media, public relations, and related marketing services. We create exciting corporate functions, festivals, events, custom programs, and innovative marketing services to meet your business needs and involve community-based programs and local affairs.

SPAs—The spa industry is another luxury category where you will benefit with general marketing, sponsorship sales, video productions, advertising, social media, public relations, blogs and related programs. Increase your exposure by participating at corporate functions, festivals, events and other community-based programs with Jean Criss Media's innovative marketing services. Preview the sites and sample promotions available to help reach your target market.

FASHION | APPAREL—A future fashion and apparel line is under development for key clientele. Jean Criss has always been a fashionista at heart, with a passion for style and high-end fashion she intends to adapt her ideas into fashion-wear. There will be more to announce in apparel **coming soon!**

©Marty Bucella   www.martybucella.com

"To tell you the truth, I don't think the average consumer will notice. Run with it."

Jean Criss also sets out to inspire others by bringing her stories to life in the **TRILOGY SERIES:** *My Pain Woke Me Up*. This series is based on survivorship—inspired by passion, perseverance, promise, and persistence. Jean learned what it takes to get knocked down by life's punches, how to get back up and the silver lining among life's difficult challenges—driven by the tales of her pursuit for happiness and the road ahead. As a breast cancer survivor, Jean creates an exciting, fashionable apparel line for health and wellness, celebrating life! with Jean Criss™ and CRISSCROSS™ brands. For more information contact us at info@ JeanCrissMedia.com.

Jean Criss Media Has Legs!

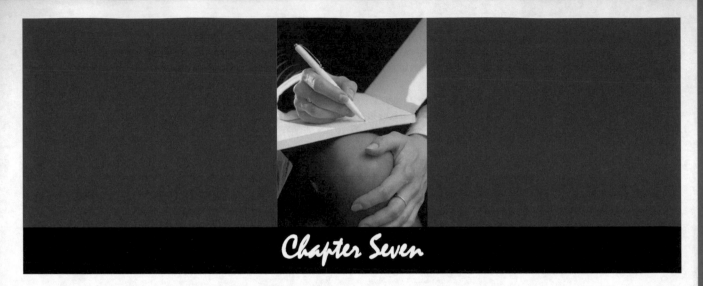

Chapter Seven

PARTNERING
(Implementation phase)

I have always been great at networking and developing strong client relations. Whether at a chamber event, women's entrepreneur meeting, or other social meetings, I make my way around the room to network. I've sustained client relations over the years from state to state, from high-tech to media, and in my personal life and in business. I'm most proud to live by 'customer first' strategies as a way of servicing my clientele. I listen to their business needs and deliver solution sets to meet those with unsurpassed and innovative creative media services.

I aspire to live, learn, laugh and love. Image your dream, create your happiness, live your life. Well I call this the let's do it phase, partner with other resources to help make your Dream happen!

* * *

Here's a great poem I found that I've enjoyed . . .

"Find a passion and pursue it. LIFE. Fall in Love. Dream BIG. Drink wine, eat great food and spend quality time with good friends. Laugh everyday. Believe in magic. Tell stories. Reminisce about the good old days but look with optimism to the future. Travel often. Learn more. Be creative. Spend time with people you admire. Seize opportunities when they reveal themselves. Love with all your heart. Never give up. Do what you love. Be true to who you are. Make time to enjoy the simple things in life. Spend time with family. Forgive even when it's hard. Smile often. Be grateful. Be the change you wish to see in the world. Follow

your dreams. Try new things. Work hard. Don't count the minutes count the laughs. Embrace change. Trust in yourself. Be thankful. Be nice to everyone. Be happy. LIVE for today. And above all . . . Make every moment count."

LIVE Your Dreams.

* * *

Another one poem in which I love and have used throughout my sales career which has inspired me goes like this;

> *"Commitment to Excellence . . . Take fast and make it faster. Take smart and make it brilliant. Believe that no matter how well you do something, you can always do it better. And chances are you will. Success. Success lies in doing. Not what others consider to be great but what you consider to be right."*

LIVE Your Dreams.

* * *

I have learned to ask questions and not to be afraid to bring in resources whenever necessary. I chose to partner with top notch companies that I admire based on the quality of their service, attention to detail, based on technologies, products and services, and former and new business relationships. I've known to do business with those that I trust. Whether a printer, technical IT expert, graphics designer, freelancer, producer, actor, voice-over specialist, illustrator, ghost-writer, lawyers of all sorts, financial planner, digital media expert, or whatever the "biz au jour", I had a few stories to share and have been proud of my portfolio of services created, credentials and contacts I've maintained over the years.

I've maintained hundreds of relationships and partners connected via social media including **LinkedIN, facebook,**

Twitter, Skype, Google, YouTube, Microsoft Outlook, and others, crossing over from the Midwest to New England to the Northeast in the NYC/NJ area, plus overseas and West Coast liaisons as well. My local team has been built with people who are interested in succeeding and have an interest in our clients success and the projects we launch. I have found that if others are excited about your ventures then they will want to help you and your customers succeed. If they are not self-motivated or interested in servicing clients with positivity, they aren't the right individuals on my team. It's all about positive communications, both intra and extra-communications.

I kept a strong list of partners and built a name for myself and have a solid group of resources to tap. Don't be afraid to lean on them for the right reasons to bring them in, when appropriate. You will find your partners and welcome those opportunities. I engage with many all the time! As a creative media services company offering a robust list of portfolio services, it was the smartest way for me to deliver client solutions in a timely manner. I have utilized resources wisely, like my entertainment attorney, as a great example, he is one leader on my team as we work with other specialists to tap or explore new ground or areas of expertise. That is how I have structured many things along the way to stay organized in front of the gate.

Meanwhile I don't lose sight of my goals and objectives and those of my client's and that's all that matters. Think of it as 1) managing multiple P&Ls and projects and 2) having multiple resources working on your team but the beauty of it is that you have low overhead. Nice!

This is how I've leveraged and implemented my business partnerships. Pragmatic, sensible, resourceful, smart business consulting the way I view it! It has worked for me thus far and I've created a network of friendships by managing this way. **SMART**—**$**uccessful— **M**anageable —**A**pproachable—**R**esourceful—**T**echnology-driven. I've applied best practices throughout my day-to-day operations as I continue to grow and uncover new ground. I thrive on new media and fresh ideas and those that inspire me.

It is not your customer's job to remember you.

It is your obligation and responsibility to make sure they don't have the chance to forget you.

- Patricia Fripp

Chapter Eight

PLAY
(Marketing, Promotion & Operation phase)

As the strategy became more refined so did all my "BIG" ideas. Each one was put into PLAY within the first 12-18 months as an entrepreneur. I utilized my sales skills and devised marketing, promotions and operations for each line of business.

First, in digital media, as my heart and soul, what I knew best. Then, with all my new ideas which I believed in, I knew I could make those dreams come true. From experiential, culinary—food, wine, spirits, to luxury and entertainment, fashion and apparel, as a new author to publishing, music and beyond, I planned, educated, researched, executed, multi-tasked, created, designed, product patents, hired consultants, lawyers, marketing experts, graphics designers, etc. basically to invest in an entire strategy that would be rolled out one phase at a time. I started one line at a time. What I didn't realize was that I surprised myself in the process—I enjoyed it so much—I moved fast—I learned from my mistakes—and made numerous products happen all at once! I was exhilarated. I multi-tasked and worked many of these projects all at the same time.

Disappointed not to bring in the dough at first, but as a close friend once told me,. . ."at the beginning of this process, it may take minimum 3 years to launch successfully as an entrepreneur with one product, so be patient", and he was right. Here I was launching about 6-10 initiatives all at once and am approaching year three since the official launch of the company and website. Nothing to be ashamed of especially with all of the projects underway—the PLAY has been amazing thus far!

Now it was time to promote and to begin the go-to-market phase/approach. Let's discuss this now.

I had learned so much over the years in sales and marketing, sure, I was anxious to advertise and successfully promote my products. However, I was conscientious and wanted to do this the right way. I had promoted companies from F25 to F500 (Fortune 25-500) and small/local businesses over the years, I felt comfortable with my business strategy.

What was funny, when I sat down with female entrepreneurs like so many of us do, we were all moving so fast, many moving parts, leveraging our resources and connections, that I found some women leaders without the traditional 3-5 year written business plan.

Well, I was no different. No marketing plan per se. We laughed about it. But honestly, do you need the written plan to market your company? Of course you don't. You can spend money any day but you should have a plan? I had a plan but it was outlined and moving and changing up frequently as I continued to grow. Does everyone really know where you will be in 5 years? May be or maybe not. Do you have an idea of where you'd like to be? Of course, do you want to share that with anyone yet? Is it necessary? No, maybe. If you aren't seeking funding, to be profitable yet, applying for a loan, etc., why waste precious time on mundane paperwork like writing a business plan? Well, the other side of the story could be . . . if you drop dead tomorrow, shouldn't someone else know your strategy and business plans? I actually interviewed for a corporate contract job, and the top executive died. While I was waiting to hear about the next steps for this contract, I knew I was the top of two candidates and that he was the final decision maker. He held the budget and info on a corporate re-org/re-structuring and since it was not written down, HR and the entire media team went scrambling and it basically shut down any movement with the project and new-hires for over 12 months at this top cable company. The death toll took more than one life, in my opinion. It impaired a billion dollar company for lack of knowledge-sharing at a high-level organization when basic, fundamental business planning should have been well documented. Instead it stunted their ability to grow in an ever so competitive marketplace of new media.

I also experienced this first hand with my first husband's death, without a will or estate plans in place. Immediately upon his death, and at my youthful age of 28 years old, I created those files for myself, even with a small estate, I knew the consequences for my future family and it was a difficult time to experience dealing with so many parties but I didn't want to burden anyone later in life and just wanted to be prepared, at whatever age. I recall colleagues in my circle at my technology company just could not relate to anything I was going thru as a young widow at that time but it didn't matter—I had experienced death at a young age and was going to learn from it and grow as a person, and that's what I did. I inherited a lot of debt from my first husband and pulled myself out of it and did not want to go thru this again or to leave my children in a bad financial situation should a terrible accident occur down the road. I learned to live my life but to be prepared, as much as one could be and to be conservative in my spending and investing. That has paid off over the years.

So I prepared to cover all those bases with my business by starting the process with the proper legal documents for everything. Using NDAs (mutual non-disclosures), invoices, SOWs (Scope of Agreements), designing a provisional and utility patent, designs patent, creating prototypes, writing books, utilizing proper trademarks and copyright laws, and other initiatives like that which involved legal advice. So the process began and was lengthy and required an education on my part and learning curve but was well worth it in the long-run. It is a much more complicated process than your simple 10-page marketing business plan. I got to work and it was time-consuming. Wow, it was time-consuming and then some! Then I realized I needed to focus on marketing promotions and not just the business basics.

That's when I hired the right partners to help me promote my products and company. I knew a lot about press relations and how to leverage media having sold and managed this process for a number of years, so I decided to test it myself. I hired a few companies to help me grow my business.

For those who believe, no proof is necessary.
For those who don't believe, no proof is possible.
-STUART CHASE-

Partner and use outside resources to help you become successful . . .

I began by hiring smart business partners. I researched those companies, talked to company references, looked at their client lists, and met with them in person. I looked at how they conducted business and basically got to know them before we started work with them. Early on in my career, I often had clients test software as an alpha or beta test site, and in the media industry had a few of the same with new technologies, and in new media, decided if a new partner was on my budget and there was reason for hesitation, we should proceed with caution to be sure that everyone is on the same page. It doesn't mean that it's a negative rather that it may take a little more time to work through the logistics of how you want the ultimate partnership to be aligned. It's actually better for both parties in the long run as they will both be in agreement for the scope of work to be completed. So I proceeded with a trial period with select partners, and longer term agreements with others. And for some, these were your short-term or one-project agreements, which is fine too. I conceded, as long as everyone delivered and was on time, life was good.

©Marty Bucella   www.martybucella.com

"The Corporate Accounting Manager position has been filled, but we do have an opening for someone who likes to forward those funny e-mails."

The best way to determine your needs is by surveying your client. I learned this early on in my career, at my first job I believe. This may have been at Wang Labs and H-P (Hewlett Packard) during pre-sales training and it stuck with me. I learned from business colleagues and friends by attending industry events, chamber meetings, and at entrepreneurial events, not to drive myself crazy, rather because each program offered a different set of deliverables and I networked and learned at each one.

Nothing is more valuable than personal relationships. Find your area of specialty, network, and use it to your business advantage. You'll learn to be a resource and invaluable coach if applied properly.

What also became important was to stay ahead of the curve—the S-curve as noted by co-authors, Whitney Johnson and her colleague Juan Carlos Mendez-Garcia.

"Just as understanding the S-curve can keep discouragement at bay as we build new knowledge, it can also help us understand why ennui kicks in once we reach the plateau. As we approach mastery, our learning rate decelerates, and while the ability to do something automatically implies competence, it also means our brains are now producing less of the feel-good neurotransmitters—the thrill ride is over.

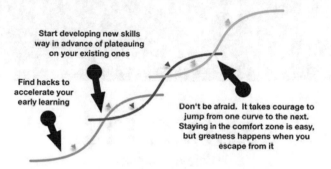

As our learning crests, should we fail to jump to new curves, we may actually precipitate our own decline. That doesn't necessarily mean a financial downfall, but our emotional and social well-being will take a hit. Saul Kaplan, Chief Catalyst at Business Innovation Factory, shares: "My life has been about searching for the steep learning curve because that's where I do my best work. When I do my best work, money and stature have always followed." Or paraphrasing James Allworth, "Steve Jobs solved the innovator's dilemma because his focus was never on profit, but better and better products." Forget the plateau of profits: seek and scale a learning curve.

The S-curve mental model makes a compelling case for personal disruption. We may be quite adept at doing the math around our future when things are linear, but neither business nor life is linear, and ultimately what our brain needs, even requires, is the dopamine of the unpredictable. More importantly, as we inhabit an increasingly zig-zag world, the best curve you can throw the competition is your ability to leap from one learning curve to the next."

This post was co-authored with Juan Carlos Mendez-Garcia, managing director of
8020world. Born in Colombia, he has lived and worked in Asia, Europe, and the United States. Juan Carlos holds an
MBA from MIT Sloan, a Masters in Systems Engineering and Bachelors on Electrical Engineering.

Source: http://blogs.hbr.org/2012/09/throw-your-life-a-curve/

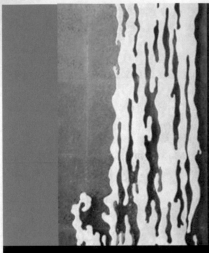

The critical ingredient is getting off your butt and doing something. It's as simple as that. A lot of people have ideas, but there are few who decide to do something about them now. Not tomorrow. Not next week. But today. The true entrepreneur is a doer, not a dreamer.

- Nolan Bushnell

Chapter Nine

LIVE IT!
(Enjoyment phase)

I took a chance and lived my dreams. I learned. I became a sponge. It's evolution at its best. Exhilaration. The enjoyment phase—Live it! But remember the true entrepreneur is a doer, not a dreamer. It's about the execution and not the dream—the vision starts with the dream but the plan happens with the proper process, ingredients, and execution.

Just as I wrote in ***BLISS!***, "**Don't Let Cancer Get the BREAST of You!**" I did not let life or anything stand in my way. I challenged myself and conquered things. I continue to explore and to push myself to new limits and levels. I enjoy it immensely.

I have traveled and written my best, seated on air planes, at poolside, simply lounging while away on vacation in my hotel room with an early morning cup of coffee or late evening glass of white wine. I cherish my children and my surroundings. The fresh air of the outdoors seated on my back deck. The love and inspiration my children bring to my life gives me pride and joy. The peace and happiness they bring inspires me to ***LIVE My Dreams***.

I was grateful to be blessed with two beautiful children. I still have my loving parents who are still kicking strong and living life to its fullest, as best as they can on their own. I visit them frequently and help them in anyway, and remain focused and supportive as any loving daughter can be.

This past summer, I appreciated a moment while out at the retail grocery store with my Dad. The check-out salesperson acknowledged us and said, "How nice of your daughter to help you Sir". It meant the world to me to hear that. As an entrepreneur, we often no longer receive praise from anyone in the workplace, but on that day to hear this from a stranger, who noticed something so personal. It wasn't about the work rather it was just extra special to hear her notice my involvement spending time with Dad, which has meant so much to me! I realized that the words I used to hear in the corporate world were less meaningful as they felt 'half-baked' most times from insincere people who were probably told to say things rather from their heart. I had outgrown my last employer when I was told everything I had to do many things such as; what to tell my employees, how they had to spent their time and how to track their time, and I could not use my own ingenuity to be creative in the corporate workplace. It was then when I realized they didn't know what they were missing and what talent they had on board—in the end, it was their loss, and not mine, in my opinion. It was obvious the people who were less sincere were the ones who were less heartfelt and empathetic. While I made close friendships with many over the years and continue some who made a difference in my life; others, well, they weren't friends to begin with. If they chose not to keep in touch for silly reasons or speculation, then they weren't worth continued relations. As I mentioned, I learned to focus on positive people in life and those who provide words of encouragement. True **BLISS!** I learned to de-friend any fears and spoke with courage from my heart.

* * *

In life, we need to make the magic happen, remember. What you are doing is most likely for your family or a loved one. I am creating my enterprise for my children so they can have a future. We live our lives to their fullest. We stop to smell the roses. We live our dreams. Don't let anyone tell you, you can't live your dreams. If they do, run the other way. Don't be held back.

Nothing is like the gratitude you can receive in return from a loved one, with love, support, appreciation of you and your work. Support non-profit charities and organizations that make a difference to you, if you can. I've learned to do so throughout my life and will continue to support organizations that make a difference to me. Give back thru fundraising, volunteering, and you will find they will give back to you as well. It's a win/win. It doesn't have to be just one-sided. If you feel it is, walk down the street and work with another non-profit organization. There are over 100,000 non-profit organizations worldwide and you can search for them and raise money while living your life with this one (www.goodsearch.com) renamed <u>Daily Good</u>®. Here are some of my favorite give-back organizations http://jeancrissmedia.com/affiliations/.

* * *

Yes, life is good. I'm in a different place for sure. I spent years "craving" the team leadership, competitive sales environment and felt the switch to a more personal side. I think this has been a huge turning point in my life. My career choices, family upbringing, young widowhood, former marriage, corporate employers, structure and policies made me a smarter business woman with solid management and leadership skills that I can apply to my own business, new markets and clientele. I can focus on small businesses, local companies, national or international firms of preference who appreciate the qualities of my areas of expertise, and have a sense of business and respect in the workplace.

All the knock down punches in life have helped me pull myself back up off the mat, as described in *BLISS!*. It's funny how you don't realize a lot about yourself until you go thru life's experiences and write them down.

As a media-preneur, engaged to apply best practices to our work and in life, and to help others succeed in their future! I enjoy being creative and working on innovative solutions to help grow various industries. I've worked in many business categories and have applied my integrated sales and marketing skills to create and produce effective programs for my clientele. I welcome new opportunities that allow us to grow and collaborate to enhance one's experiential customer engagement.

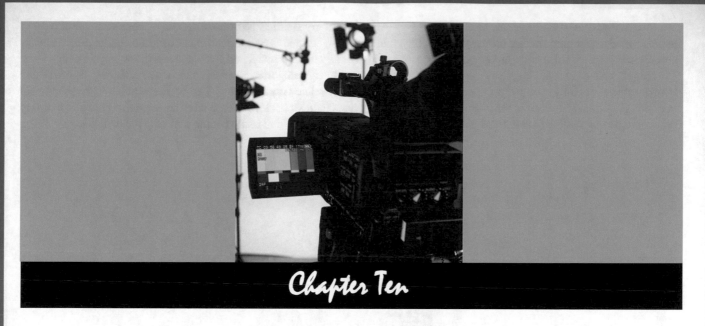

Chapter Ten

ENJOY IT!
(Profitable phase)

It's time to live it! That's what I said anyway. So I did it. I am, and I'm living it!!

I've outlined new media ideas, applied what I've learned from my **Beaded Baubles, LLC** days, corporate world days to my new world of digital media, culinary and luxury, and am engaged in an ever so diverse set of multi-media mix. I always worked in integrated sales and marketing, and publishing in my early digital media and tech days and that's why I believe I was able to craft such a robust enterprise—a product line of various industry categories, reaching numerous marketing segments and demographics, touching non-profit organizations and various cause-related organizations. I combined a little of everything that I've been passionate about over the years. During my first 25 years in business I've attempted to package this portfolio in a way that would be marketable to mass audiences. My only hope is that it will be and many people will reap the benefits.

GLASBERGEN
© Randy Glasbergen / glasbergen.com

"Look at the bright side. After we outsource your job,
if you get fired, it will be somebody else!"

I was in the "enjoy it" phase and now look forward to the profitable phase where many of these products and services are marketable and available. It is time to make some moolah!

I'm connecting with the "sharks" of ABC's award-winning entrepreneurs on Shark Tank and leveraging the "ladies" and "women- preneurs" to engage the best of the best with my actionable next steps.

I told myself I should be a 'lady prowess.' To me, that meant be conservative, respectful and a reserved woman entrepreneur. I knew what I would need to do should I hit a bump in the road and to simply tailor or adjust your plan accordingly. Now let's drive in ease and ride that road in pursuit to happiness. It's a great feeling of success—to deliver all of these services after all the effort and planning that has gone into them.

I bring in outside resources on a project by project basis and have learned that is the best way to manage a growing boutique agency—low overhead and low expenses. Initially I had hired a few marketing staff and all my money was going toward supporting them versus paying myself. I learned the hard way that you need to pay yourself and your bills first before expanding to pay others. I've had many business women want to partner with me and share office expenses and office space, I politely decline. I don't want to incur additional expenses or get in over my head. Someday when I can afford to have that discretionary income, I will be able to make those decisions and it's a great feeling knowing that others will want to share office space, support people and technologies with you as you grow and expand. It's all about doing the right things while you are in growth mode and keeping your head above the water is the main focus. I continue to focus on my priorities and not those of others businesses. If someone is not interested in paying for my services, I've learned to move on to the next lead. I qualify faster and get thru my survey process in a more expeditious manner to make smart business decisions. That continues to help me grow and expand my business relations. Keeping focused is the name of the game and knowing when to bring in a partner is also critical to strategic planning and your success, I've learned. Don't be afraid to say 'No' or 'Yes' when the time is right!

I was inspired by positive psychologist and author, Dr. Barbara Becker Holstein after I first read her material on *The Enchanted Self*. Then after months of attempting to meet-up, we finally did succeed and it was a **BLISS**-ful day!

As co-authors, we shared one another's books, stories, successes and upcoming events and engaged in discussion how to collaborate.

BLISS! and **LIVE Your Dreams** seemed like a nice fit with *The Enchanted Self* and *Secrets* so we devised a series of speaking engagements, radio talk shows and ways to collaborate.

That's how it's done—women working well with one another— finding common meeting ground and ways to support each other. We look forward to putting this into PLAY and to our ride this Spring/ Summer 2014!

I would like to highlight a few notable points from Dr. Holstein's *Seven Gateways to Happiness: Freeing Your Enchanted Self*. "To obtain true happiness we must go through all the Gateways at one time or another in your life. You recognize all of them as essential parts as being alive.

The Seven Gateways to Happiness are in order that goes from where we often have to start as Women and finish where we long to be as competent adults. It is also a structure that can be named and changed as suits each women's needs. You may even find yourself in two or three Gateways at once or see that once you start in one Gateway in order to continue growing, you must tap into another."

© Randy Glasbergen
glasbergen.com

"We're outsourcing your bathroom breaks to a person in another country."

© Randy Glasbergen
www.glasbergen.com

"My boyfriend and I aren't ready to move in together, but we've started keeping our data on the same cloud."

1. Self Esteem—where values of thoughts, talents, memories and potential, feelings about our purpose in life, coping skills, dreams and desires.

2. Emotional Gut Level—Falling in love, flaws and mistakes.

3. Learning how to meet our needs—negotiate for ourselves, facilitate a life.

4. Pleasure & Rejuvenation—gateway of love!

5. Belonging—keeps us from isolation and depression

6. Mentoring & Wisdom—knowledge to pass on to others

7. Positive Action & Good Deed—bridges to spiritual, dignity, events which help us experience happiness . . . Research validates that the giver benefits emotionally from giving. So soon you'll be on the road to happiness!"

BLISS!

Each day I continue to juggle different things and that is okay. I find the most challenging continues to be my local IT issues, and working from the home office has had its pluses and minuses too. I broke new ground earlier this year by opening up a part-time office in the city to expand my business and that was a great choice for me. While I continue to grow my LLC, I look forward to new opportunities and horizon points.

LIVE Your Dreams**!**

I've learned to stay positive and to avoid people and places that draw any negative attention. I've spent so much time reaching for the sky—where that's been the limit. I learned how to ***LIVE My Dreams***!

Don't stop when opportunity comes knocking at your door. Reach for that sky. Find it, embrace it, better yet, create it!

My new world of ***LIVE Your Dreams*** was all about experiencing life's greatest moments and surrounding myself with those that inspire me. Being positive was the key to continuing on with my dreams. I learned a lot about the effects of negative energy from insincere individuals, co- dependence, and depression arising from breast cancer, multiple surgeries, a broken marriage and unemployment in one fell swoop. I committed to never let my mind body and soul go there again if I could help it. A woman of determination I have always been. Driven by self-motivation, strong values, and taught by some great business leaders and my wonderful parents—my father who has been so endearing to me and one of the greatest leaders I've ever known. My dad taught me to be a multi-tasking entrepreneur. After all, he successfully worked numerous jobs for over six decades! As a general dentist, builder, developer, realtor, landlord, professional pianist, and awesome father of four, husband and grandfather to five and my mother who taught me about leadership as a woman, the world of multi-tasking women and family, and motherhood at large. I am grateful to have learned from both of them and to apply what I believe have been solid values to my family, personal life and in the growth of my business and career, as a female entrepreneur and business woman.

I've worked for many other great leaders who inspired me, read about others in awesome books and memoires, and attended numerous lectures and conferences over the years to be that "sponge". I hope my children will learn the positive things that I have shown them and use those best practices throughout their lives to help them grow and succeed just as I have. I love them so very, very much and that's what this pursuit for happiness as an entrepreneur is all about.

LIVE Your Dreams—a story about entrepreneurship—dreaming BIG—living it—and unleashing your inner creativity. Make all those dreams come true. And don't forget to "stop and smell the roses along the way too!" Can you s-m-e-l-l them yet? I do! They are robust, fragrant and beautiful.

I am a true believer in . . . 'enjoy life to its fullest good things will come'. You can make it happen for yourself too!

***LIVE Your Dreams*!**

"20 SIMPLE TIPS TO BE HAPPY NOW"

Dr. Timothy Sharp,
author of "The Happiness Handbook" Founder of The Happiness Institute
(www.thehappinessinstitute.com)

1. Make happiness a priority.
2. Make plans to be happy.
3. Set happy goals.
4. Do things that make you happy.
5. Set yourself tasks from which you'll gain satisfaction.
6. Play and have fun.
7. Identify where your strengths lie.
8. Utilize your strengths.
9. Be curious.
10. Be grateful and appreciate what you have.
11. Learn to like and ideally to love yourself.
12. Invest time and energy in to your key relationships.
13. Socialize and interact with others as much as possible.
14. Weed out unhelpful thoughts.
15. Plant happier, optimistic thoughts.
16. Live a healthier life.
17. Ensure you gain adequate sleep and rest.
18. Manage your time and priorities.
19. Control what you can control.
20. Live in the present moment.

And an EXTRA tip to make you happy!

Make happiness an integral part of your life!

The End

every STORY has an END, but in LIFE every END is just a new BEGINNING

About the Author

Jean Criss is the author of **LIVE Your Dreams**, the third book in **My Pain Woke Me Up** trilogy about how to dream BIG, live it, and unleash your inner creativity to make all those dreams come true. *BLISS!* and Legal Injustice were self-published in December, 2012. Jean wrote *LIVE Your Dreams* as a non-fiction documenting her journey as an entrepreneur who's dedicated and passionate about digital media, luxury and entertainment, culinary cuisine and the related wine and food industry, and in support of many philanthropic causes. She discusses how she became an entrepreneur early on in the jewelry business and then used her corporate experience and best practices in media and high-tech and applied them in the workplace.

All books are available in soft cover and e-book format through all major media outlets including Amazon, Barnes & Noble and AuthorHouse Publishing. You can learn more about the trilogy at http://jeancrissmedia.com/author-trilogyseries/ and purchase them at https://www.facebook.com/JeanCrissAuthor.

Jean Criss resides in Northern New Jersey with her two teenagers and works in New York City and New Jersey. Please enjoy this read. Soon there will be other exciting announcements from our author!

To note a few; **6-Figures** is a leading international professional business organization to engage highly accomplished women to engage in doing business differently, **Women's Leadership Exchange** or better known as **LEXCI**—is a women's leadership group which connects business woman to grow professionally on local and national levels, **Ladies Who Launch** is an entrepreneurial group coaching women in business to "Dream it, Launch it, and Live it!"; **B.I.G.** (Believe, Inspire, Grow) is a community based women's organization, and there are others that Jean's affiliated with.

Professional affiliations include *NY WIFT* (NY International Film and Television Bureau) where she sits on both the programming and communications committees for the annual Designing Women and MUSE Awards, *WICTV* (Women in Cable TV) and *CAB* (Cable Advertising TV Bureau) , marketing resources for her industry, and dozens of local chambers throughout the region. She is also involved with the *James Beard Foundation*, an organization dedicated to celebrate, nurture, and honor America's diverse culinary heritage through programs that educate and inspire. There are other industry affiliations she works closely with that empower women and that she makes the effort to be involved with across her areas of specialty.

Jean resides in Northern New Jersey with her two teenagers and very much enjoys writing as an entrepreneur. You can learn more about the trilogy series *My Pain Woke Me Up* at http:// jeancrissmedia.com/author-trilogyseries/ and can purchase her books at https://www.facebook.com/JeanCrissAuthor.

Printed in the United States
By Bookmasters